# THE CHRISTIAN
# hall of fame

ELMER L. TOWNS

BAKER BOOK HOUSE &bull; Grand Rapids, Michigan 49506

# *Introduction*

The Christian Hall of Fame was born in my mind as I lay in Aultman Hospital recovering from a heart attack which I experienced in November, 1964. After reading the 11th chapter of Hebrews, I heard a radio announcement referring to the Professional Football Hall of Fame which is located in our city. The idea came to me that we should put "God's Heroes" on display in our church: the men who through the centuries have stood for the faith once and for all delivered to the saints. The following Christian artists were commissioned to paint the original oil portraits: Dr. Peter Ruckman of Pensacola, Florida; Dr. Harold Wittig of Ramsey, New Jersey; Mr. Carl Blair and Mr. Emory Bopp, members of the Art Faculty of Bob Jones University, Greenville, South Carolina; Mrs. Shirley Henly of Tennessee Temple Schools, Chattanooga, Tennessee; and Mrs. Evelyn Carter of Monroe, Michigan.

The Christian Hall of Fame is designed to trace the progress of Biblical Christianity from the closing of the New Testament Canon down through the centuries until this present hour. Among these men are early church fathers, reformers, missionaries, pastors, scholars, and evangelists. Though differing in background, education, method, and field of ministry, these men had in common an unswerving devotion to the Lord Jesus Christ and a complete dedication to His Word.

The main purpose of the Christian Hall of Fame is inspirational, not merely educational. It is our prayer that as a result of viewing the likenesses of these men and reading the biographies, many will be inspired to carry the blood-stained banner of the cross around the world as missionaries; that men will be called into the ministry to preach the unsearchable riches of Christ; and that all will be led to a life dedicated to the honor of Him who loved us and washed us from our sins in His own blood, even our Lord Jesus Christ. To Him be the glory. To that end this volume is dedicated.

HAROLD HENNIGER, D.D.
Pastor, Canton Baptist Temple

# Contents

# Preface

There is no such thing as an average Christian. Every believer has a unique contribution to invest for God. Every believer can respond to the challenge as did Esther. Though insignificant, she was asked, "Who knoweth whether thou art come to the kingdom for such a time as this?" (Esther 4:14). Every faithful believer deserves a place in God's Hall of Fame.

But there are powerful men of God . . . influential men of God . . . those who rise above mediocrity and turn the tide of history. These are enshrined in The Christian Hall of Fame, located in the Canton Baptist Temple, Canton, Ohio. They are outstanding heroes of faith who have stood alone against sin, many giving their blood, others counting no sacrifice too great. Some have swayed the decisions of kings; others have moved the hearts of the masses. Some have quietly diverted the course of history through the power of the written page; others have stood in the lecture hall and inflamed the minds of students to go out and win the multitudes for God. Some were great orators of Biblical truth; however, one is even known to have stuttered when he spoke. Each person enshrined in The Christian Hall of Fame has been used of God, some to a greater degree than others. But all have been unusually successful in the investment of their lives for God.

Most Sunday school students will have heard the names of Martin Luther and John Wesley, but may not have heard the names of Lewis Sperry Chafer, Savonarola, or H. C. Morrison, yet their lives are considered influential for the cause of Christ, even though they themselves have little fame. All must stand to give an account before the judgment seat of Christ — the well known and the unknown — where the acclaims of men will be forgotten and each will receive his reward for his work upon earth.

The honor brought by our remembrance of these *Men of God* will grant them no merit when they stand before God. But each enshrinee, though dead, will continue to live through the influence of The Christian Hall of Fame. As you view the portraits and read of the exploits of each man of God, may you be challenged to greater service.

Canton Baptist Temple has a Sunday school of over 4,700 students. The August, 1970 issue of *Christian Life* magazine revealed it had the fastest growing Sunday school in the United States. Once, when visiting this thriving Sunday school, I observed Dr. Harold Henniger and three junior boys walk slowly before the majestic portraits in The Christian Hall of Fame. Pointing to Dwight L. Moody, Dr. Henniger remarked, "I'd like for one of you boys to be a greater soul winner than he was." The group stopped before the piercing eyes of Savonarola. Again the pastor spoke to the students: "I hope none of you boys have to be burned before the stake as this great preacher was." The boys didn't respond, but their eyes indicated the lessons were being absorbed as the pastor and his young boys continued their stroll before the great heroes of faith.

Later Dr. Henniger stated, "If The Christian Hall of Fame can inspire some of our young boys to do exploits for God, we will have accomplished its purpose." Maybe they will, for young boys strive to imitate the heroes they admire.

My heart was greatly moved as I read hundreds of sermons and writings of the men in this volume. An attempt was made to choose the sermon or writing that would best reflect the heart and influence of the man. Further selection had to be made, for inclusion of complete sermons would have made too large a book. The goal was to give brief insight into the life and ministry of each man, stating his qualifications for inclusion into The Christian Hall of Fame. Excerpts from sermons or writings do not accompany every biographical sketch because an attempt was made to keep the volume concise for reading ease and inexpensive for broader coverage. If your favorite sermon is not included, or if we have not included a sermon from a man of God who influenced you, we ask your indulgence.

Several contributors to The Christian Hall of Fame and this volume should be noted. An original financial grant from the estate of Mr. and Mrs. Raymond Parks made The Christian Hall of Fame possible. Reverend Robert Johnson, assistant to the pastor of Canton Baptist Temple, did the original research for each portrait and biography appearing in The Christian Hall of Fame. Mr. Glen Miller and Mr. John Fisher, graduate assistants, Trinity Evangelical Divinity School, Deerfield, Illinois, also did research for this volume. I am indebted to them for finding original writings of the enshrinees that some thought couldn't be found.

As you read these pages I have a three-fold prayer, that your:

*minds* be fascinated with accomplishments that can still be accomplished for God;

*emotions* be stirred to greater worship of God and enthusiasm for daily service;

*will* be surrendered for God's purpose.

ELMER L. TOWNS

# PART I

# THE APOSTOLIC CHURCH

## *From Christ to A.D. 500*

One of the most amazing events in history is the tremendous expansion of Christianity during its first five centuries. It started as a seemingly obscure movement, one among many in the Roman world, but it was carried by the apostles to the known world. Rome first tried to contain Christianity and later to destroy it through severe persecution, but Christianity eventually grew to the extent that being a Roman citizen was almost identical with being a Christian. The Christian Church won the professed allegiance of the great majority of the Roman Empire, as well as the support of the Roman state.

During this period the church developed a visible organization and formulated a system of beliefs. The growth of these two factors were interrelated. By the time the majority of the Empire had adopted Christianity, the main features of the structure of the Christian community and its major verbal expressions, the Apostles' and Nicene Creeds had been established. Standards for admission to the church were being set; forms of worship were developing; discipline for maintaining Christian standards of life were being devised.

Beginning in the third century, questions concerning the proper way to live the Christian life were raised, since there appeared a relaxation of Christian standards and a widening gap between the ideal and the actual Christian. Monasticism arose out of this context, partially as a rebellion by the individual against the organization of the Church. These laymen who lived alone were at first looked down on by Church authorities, but their movement spread so that by the fifth century monasticism was a dominant characteristic of the Church.

During this period, Christianity faced several perils. There was a belief in the sharp disjunction between the spiritual and material worlds, followed by a temptation to regard Christianity as a philosophy, somewhat similar to Greek philosophy. Pride of position and desire for control of church machinery began to characterize many church officials. Christians began to participate in the social life of the Empire in a way often inconsistent with their commitment.

In summary, many considered themselves Christians but few really were. The Church adapted itself to accommodate the unsaved. Local churches were engulfed by organization. There was a growth in the wealth, prestige and power of the clergy, strengthened by the bestowal of civil power. The whole period was one of theological vigor and expansion of membership.

11

# *Ignatius*

## (35–107)

Ignatius was the Bishop of Antioch, where disciples were first called Christians (Acts 11). He was a native Syrian and an "eyewitness" to the apostles, a friend of John the beloved apostle, and a contemporary of Polycarp. Ignatius was the first man to use the term *Catholic*, but he never used the term in any letter referring to anything more than the body of born-again believers who were planted in Christ by the Holy Spirit. At no time did Ignatius suggest that the word *Catholic* be applied to anything Roman or associated with Rome, nor did he connect it with anyone who thought water baptism was a part of salvation.

The attitude of Ignatius was reflected in the statement, "I would rather die for Christ than rule the whole earth. Leave me to the beasts that I may by them be a partaker of God . . . welcome nails and cross, welcome broken bones, bruised body, welcome all diabolic torture, if I may but obtain the Lord Jesus Christ." Ignatius was thrown to the lions and eaten alive in A.D. 107.

While under guard on a journey to Rome on the way to martyrdom, he wrote several letters to churches in Asia Minor, and stressed the continuation of the Church under the pastor (bishop) after his death.

## From His Letter to the Ephesians

*And pray ye without ceasing in behalf of other men. For there is in them hope of repentance that they may attain to God. See, then, that they be instructed by your works, if in no other way. Be ye meek in response to their wrath, humble in opposition to their boasting: to their blasphemies return your prayers; in contrast to their error, be ye stedfast in the faith; and for their cruelty, manifest your gentleness. While we take care not to imitate their conduct, let us be found their brethren in all true kindness; and let us seek to be followers of the Lord (who ever more unjustly treated, more destitute, more condemned?) that so no plant of the devil may be found in you, but ye may remain in all holiness and sobriety in Jesus Christ, both with respect to the flesh and spirit.*

# Polycarp

## (69–155)

Polycarp, who lived the first generation after the apostles, was born in Smyrna and later became the bishop of the city. He was a disciple of the apostle John and also a friend of Ignatius. Polycarp was a dedicated student of the Pauline Epistles and the Gospel of John. He had little to say about sacraments or ritual. He maintained that each church was independent of any outside human authority. He never referred to the ministers as priests, and he never taught that water baptism had anything to do with salvation. He was the last survivor of those who had talked with the eyewitnesses of Jesus. As a very old man he was arrested, tried, and condemned. When asked to renounce his faith in Christ, he replied, "Eighty-six years have I served him and he hath done me no wrong. How can I speak evil of my king who saved me?" Polycarp was burned alive, and when, according to tradition, the flames refused to consume him, he was killed with the sword and then burned.

## From a Letter Addressed to the Philippians

*"But the love of money is the root of all evils." Knowing, therefore, that "as we brought nothing into the world, so we can carry nothing out," let us arm ourselves with the armour of righteousness; and let us teach, first of all, ourselves to walk in the commandments of the Lord. Next, [teach] your wives [to walk] in the faith given to them, and in love and purity, tenderly loving their own husbands in all truth, and loving all [others] equally in all chastity; and to train up their children in the knowledge and fear of God. Teach the widows to be discreet as respects the faith of the Lord, praying continually for all, being far from all slandering, evil-speaking, false-witnessing, love of money, and every kind of evil; knowing that they are the altar of God, that He clearly perceives all things, and that nothing is hid from Him, neither reasonings, nor reflections, nor any one of the secret things of the heart.*

# Quintus Florens Tertullian

## (160–220)

Tertullian was born of pagan parents in Carthage, Africa. He studied law and lived a sinful life until he received the Lord Jesus Christ at the age of thirty. Although he gave no clear reason why he turned to Christianity, it is evident that his observation of the martyrdom of Christians influenced his life. He commented, "Everyone, in the face of such prodigious endurance, feels himself as it were struck by some doubt, and ardently desires to find out what there is at the bottom of this matter: from the moment that he understands the truth, he forthwith embraces it himself."

Tertullian became an intense defender of the Christian faith against the traditions of Romanism both in its teachings and practices. He joined the Montanists, a sect that rigorously held to ethical purity in contrast to the evils in the Church of the day.

In A.D. 197 he wrote his famous *Apologeticus* and also *Ad Nationes*. The latter was an attack on pagan morals and beliefs, while the former was a defense of the morals and beliefs of the Christians. He spent the rest of his life writing and preaching primitive Christianity, emphasizing separation and fighting worldliness in the Church.

## From the Sermon,
## "The Duty and Benefits of Patience"

*In this world we carry about us our very souls and bodies exposed to injury from all men, and under this injury we submit to be patient. Shall we be grieved by taking thought for things of lesser moment? Away with such defilement from the servant of Christ, that his patience, made ready for greater temptations, should fall away in trifling ones. If any shall try to provoke thee by open violence, the admonition of the Lord is at hand*: To him that smiteth thee on the face, saith He, turn the other cheek also. *Let his wickedness be wearied out by thy patience. Be the blow what it may, bound up with pain and insult, he will suffer a heavier one from the Lord. Thou beatest that wicked man the more by bearing with him, for he shall be beaten by Him, for whose sake thou bearest with him. If the bitterness of the tongue should break out in cursing or railing, reflect on that which hath been said*: Rejoice when men shall curse you. *The Lord Himself was cursed under the Law, and yet is the only Blessed. Wherefore let us His servants follow our Lord, and let us take cursing patiently, that we may be able to be blessed. If I hear not with unruffled mind any wanton or naughty word spoken against me, I must needs myself also render bitter speech in my turn, or I shall be tortured by silent impatience. When therefore I have smitten another with evil*

16

*speaking, how shall I be found to have followed the teaching of the Lord, wherein it is delivered unto us that a man is* defiled *not by the pollutions of* vessels, *but of* those things which proceed out of *the* mouth?

# Chrysostom (John of Antioch)

## (347–407)

John Chrysostom was born and reared in Antioch, Syria, where he studied the Scriptures and served as a deacon. During his ten-year pastorate in Antioch he taught the Scriptures and also wrote commentaries. He was made Archbishop of Constantinople in 398 and preached there for six years, condemning sin in high places as well as low places. The empress Eudoxia banished him because she said that he had insulted her. Chrysostom was soon recalled, but not tamed. He continued his strong preaching against sin until banished to the desert again, where he died. Thirty years later his bones were taken back to Constantinople and were buried during a funeral service that gave public recognition to the godly life he lived. His oratorical powers caused him to be called *Chrysostom* which means "the golden mouth."

## From the Sermon,
## "Excessive Grief at the Death of Friends"

*For on what account, tell me, do you thus weep for one departed? Because he was a bad man? You ought on that very account to be thankful, since the occasions of wickedness are now cut off. Because he was good and kind? If so, you ought to rejoice; since he has been soon removed, before wickedness had corrupted him, and he has gone away to a world where he stands ever secure, and there is no room even to mistrust a change. Because he was a youth? For that, too, praise Him that has taken him, because He has speedily called him to a better lot. Because he was an aged man? On this account, also, give thanks and glorify Him that has taken him. Be ashamed of your manner of burial. The singing of psalms, the prayers, the assembling of the [spiritual] fathers and brethren — all this is not that you may weep, and lament, and afflict yourselves, but that you may render thanks to Him who has taken the departed. For as when men are called to some high office, multitudes with praises on their lips assemble to escort them at their departure to their stations, so do all with abundant praise join to send forward, as to greater honor, those of the pious who have departed. Death is rest, a deliverance from the exhausting labors and cares of this world. When, then, thou seest a relative departing, yield not to despondency; give thyself to reflection; examine thy conscience; cherish the thought that after a little while this end awaits thee also. Be more considerate; let another's death excite thee to salutary fear; shake off all indolence; examine your past deeds; quit your sins, and commence a happy change.*

# Patrick

## (389–461)

The first missionary to Ireland, Patrick was born in Britain though the exact location is uncertain. His father was a Roman centurion and also a deacon in a local New Testament church. Patrick was taken captive at sixteen and remained in captivity for six years. During this period he tended cattle and prayed for release. He escaped from Ireland and later was converted to Christ. He studied on the mainland in Gaul with Germanus. Patrick had a vision like that of St. Paul at Troas, which called him to Ireland. This country had been much in his thoughts and prayers. Returning to the heathen tribes in Ireland as a missionary, he began scores of churches and baptized (immersed) thousands of converts. He is largely responsible for the large number of Bible-believing Christians in Northern Ireland, Scotland, and England.

Patrick, his father, and also his grandfather were proud of the fact that they were responsible only to God. Patrick was later canonized by the Roman Church as a political move to control the Irish churches. He was thereafter known as Saint Patrick.

## From Patrick's Account of His Vision

*And on another night, I know not, God knows, whether in me, or near me, with most eloquent words which I heard, and could not understand except at the end of the speech, one spoke as follows, "He who gave His life for thee is He who speaks in thee," and so I awoke full of joy. And again I saw Him praying in me, and He was as it were within my body, and I heard above me, that is, above the inner man, and there He was praying mightily with groanings. And meanwhile I was stupefied and astonished, and pondered who it could be that was praying in me. But at the end of the prayer He so spoke as if He were the Spirit. And so I awoke, and remembered that the Apostle says, "The Spirit helps the infirmities of our prayers. For we know not what we should pray for as we ought; but the Spirit Himself asketh for us with unspeakable groanings," which cannot be expressed in words. And again [he says] "The Lord is our advocate, and prays for us."*

# PART II

# THE CHURCH THROUGH THE DARK AGES

## A.D. 500 to 1000

Few religions survive beyond the cultures with which they are identified. Through its first five hundred years, Christianity had not only spread throughout the Roman Empire, but it also became identified with and integrated into its civilization. In 410 the city of Rome was burned and sacked, and in 476 the last of the Roman emperors was overthrown. By 500 the Roman Empire and its Graeco-Roman culture were in serious decline. The Empire was invaded from two directions. From the North came pagan, barbaric tribes. From the South came the Arabs, who brought with them a new and more vigorous religion, Islam. By the year 1000 the Arabs and Islam controlled one-half of what had been Roman and Christian. Christian churches dwindled rapidly in areas dominated by the Arabs.

But Christianity survived. Already in 496 Clovis, King of the Franks, was baptized. This event marked the beginning of an era in which the Germans were to be the champions of the faith in the West. So, although it lost ground in some areas, in the West Christianity eventually displayed fresh vigor and creativity.

In the sixth century Justinian I renewed much of Roman administration in the West in North Africa and added prestige to the Church in the East. It was during this century that Christianity spread into the Sudan and China. In the West Pope Gregory I added to the Church's power and sent missionaries into Britain, resulting in its conversion.

The seventh century brought on the rapid Moslem conquests. By A.D. 715 they had overrun Spain as well as the Middle East and North Africa. During those years the pagan Slavs and Bulgars moved into the Balkan and Danube River areas and established non-Christian states in formerly Christian areas.

In the eighth century there was a revival in faith and morale in the West. Much of Germany was converted, but the ninth and tenth centuries brought new invasions of pagans. They established themselves in parts of Britain and France and along the shores of Europe. The invasions brought on a decline in the quality of life of Western Christianity. Monasteries became lax, and the morals of the clergy deteriorated. The Papacy became the victim of local factions in Rome.

In the eighth and ninth centuries, the Eastern Church, with its center at Constantinople, was split by a long controversy over idols or images. The Arabs and Islam, meanwhile, had conquered Sicily and southern Italy. In China, persecution weakened the churches.

Near the end of the ninth century, Christianity advanced in Central Europe as the Byzantine Empire (Constantinople) was regaining strength. As the tenth century began, reforms started by the monastery at Cluny, France, spread through the West. The Roman Empire in the West was revived in A.D. 962 under the German, Otto I. The end of the century marked the beginning of the conversion of Russia. These were some of the signs that an upswing of Christianity was on the way.

In looking at Christianity at the end of its first millenium, one can see that the last five hundred years were years of decline. Christianity had lost ground to Islam and Confucianism geographically and culturally. This was also the period of minor divisions (sects) within Christianity. There were the Arians, Copts, Monophysites, and Nestorians in various parts of the "Christian" world. These were partly cultural divisions, but they were also partly doctrinal. During this period the two main wings (East and West) of the Catholic Church drifted apart. In spite of the darkness of these years, especially in the ninth and early tenth centuries, there were men of outstanding Christian influence. As this period drew to a close there were also signs of a reawakening.

# Columba

## (521–597)

Columba was born in Donegal, Ireland. Very little is known about his early life and education. He studied at Celtic schools and in 551 was ordained a priest. In 563, he and twelve of his followers sailed to Scotland, where he established a center of missionary activity at Iona. His labors resulted in reaching the entire island with Christianity. He founded numerous monasteries in the Hebrides and on the Scottish mainland. Tradition tells that Columba lived an ascetic life and compelled his monks to pattern their lives after his example. Neither his solitary habits (he often withdrew from the monastery into the woods for prayer) nor his absolute authority alienated his monks' affection for him.

Columba's ministry contrasted sharply with that of Augustine, who later came to Britain. Augustine represented the Roman Church while Columba was a product of the Celtic Church of Britain.

Columba is said to have been of noble appearance. He certainly had the gifts of great leadership along with marked literary tastes. Late in life he visited Ireland to attend a council at which the suppression of the bards (singing poets) was discussed. One of his favorite teachers in youth had been a bard. Columba defended the order so well that it was not suppressed, but only restricted. At Iona he spent much time in writing and made the copying of manuscripts a prominent feature of the work of the institution. The production of copies of the Scriptures and of other books for the numerous mission stations was an important part of the whole undertaking. The last work of Columba was the transcription of Scripture. On the day preceding his death he was busy transcribing the Psalms. He wrote as far as the words, "They who seek the Lord shall want no manner of thing that is good" (Psalm 34:10). At that point he said, "I think that I shall write no more." On Sunday morning, June 9, 597, he was found dead before the altar in the church.

So profound was the impression of Columba and his mission establishment on the British Islands that for many generations all the kings of Scotland were brought to Iona for burial beside their great apostle. Many historians consider his work and ministry of promoting Christianity in the British Isles far greater than that of the first "Archbishop of Canterbury."

# PART III

# THE CHURCH IN REFORMATION

## A.D. 1000 to 1500

From A.D. 1000 to 1350 Christianity won the formal religious allegiance of most of Northwestern and Central Europe. Christianity advanced into Russia and recaptured the Iberian Peninsula from Islam; was carried to Iceland, Greenland, and possibly North America. Small groups in Central, East, and South Asia professed belief. Christianity's major strength and vitality was in Western Europe.

In the East, the Byzantine Empire was gaining power. In the West, the outside invasions stopped, growth in commercial wealth occurred and modern political states were born. Commerce revived, and Europe was emerging from feudalism. This was the period of the rise of professing Christian kingdoms throughout Europe. This was also the period of the Crusades. Although this was a period of resurgence, its influence was not as great numerically as in A.D. 500 (the Christians were scattered over a wider area), yet in Europe its influence was much deeper than in Rome in A.D. 500. Islam and Buddhism, as well as Hinduism and Confucianism, were growing in influence. However, Christianity had proved that it was able to survive both the decline of its political protectors and the corruption of its own religious system.

Christianity rewon only a small portion of the land it had lost to Islam, but suffered no new losses. It entered significantly into every major phase of the new culture (life-style) emerging in Western Europe. Christianity was spreading into Eastern Europe and Russia. Even this resurgence was not completely in conformity with Biblical Christianity. However, as before, true Christianity was affecting individuals throughout this period, and it looked as if God's power was soon to be shown in a mighty way.

However, this period of resurgence (A.D. 1000-1350) was followed by another period of decline (A.D. 1350-1500). Christianity's geographic frontiers shrank greatly. It vanished from most of Asia and parts of the Balkans. There was decay in Western Europe.

In China the Ming Dynasty replaced the Mongols and hastened the disappearance of Christianity there. Tamerlane, a fanatic Moslem, carried on extensive wars of conquest through Central Asia, Persia, Mesopotamia, and North India, causing the end of Christianity in these areas.

The Ottoman Turks took much of Asia Minor from its Christian rulers. In 1452 Constantinople fell before their advance. They swept into the Balkans and Eastern Europe, bringing Islam with them.

The new age just beginning in Western Europe posed threats to Christianity. The plague of "Black Death" had wiped out many missionaries. Absolute monarchs were rising in power in the political states of Europe as the Holy Roman Empire declined. They were extending their power over the churches in their areas. Feudal society was passing from the scene. Unfortunately, the Church had been identified with it. The Renaissance, with its humanism, was spreading and undercutting much of Christianity. The men of the Renaissance (humanists) viewed man as able to determine his own destiny. They ruled out God and the supernatural. There was much scoffing at Christianity and much criticism of the Church's structure. The Eastern and Western kings of the church drifted further apart and finally split completely during these years. The monasteries, the clergy, and the Papacy were badly corrupted. Christian morality was flaunted.

Despite the grimness of the situation, it was not as bad as the decline during the Dark Ages. The main body of Christendom remained, although many Christian communities in Asia had died out. There were advances in Spain and Russia. There was also some vitality in the Church in Russia, and there was a spread of Christian mysticism in Europe along with some monastic reform. This was the period of the rise of the Brethren of the Common Life, of Wycliffe and the Lollards, of Hus and the Hussites. These were a small indication of explosive things to come.

# John Wycliffe

## (1320–1384)

Wycliffe was a Saxon, born in Hipswell, England. From Oxford University he received the doctor of theology degree in 1372. After serving as envoy to France, representing England in a dispute with the Pope, he returned to England and wrote against the secular power of the Papacy. In spite of attempts by the Church to have Wycliffe arrested and assassinated, he continued to write and preach. He maintained that no Pope or council was infallible, and that if their views contradicted the Bible, those views were wrong. He taught that the clergy should not rule as "princes of the church," but should help the people and "lead them to Christ."

No preacher ever regarded the condition of the people more sincerely or set about to help them more persistently than did John Wycliffe. Mingling among the common people, he developed an understanding for the poor. In a day when monks and friars were neglecting the ministry to the poor, Wycliffe's attitude was one of a shepherd rather than a hireling. Like Jesus in Galilee, John Wycliffe preached to the poor and lost the favor of those in high places. He opposed their blind worship of something they did not understand while the priests made their understanding darker and their ignorance greater.

Wycliffe's purpose was to bring to the common people the truth that the way of salvation lay through an understanding of spiritual light. In his preaching, he sought to develop an understanding of the Bible and its message of salvation through Jesus Christ. Convincingly he confronted his listeners with the demands of the Christian life. John Wycliffe's message was one of hope and salvation in the midst of poverty, corruption, and misery.

In answer to the question, "How must the Word of God be preached?" Wycliffe once answered, "Appropriately, simply, directly, and from a devout, sincere heart."

Finally prohibited by the Bishop of London from preaching, Wycliffe confined himself to writing and translating the Bible from Latin to English. Thirty-one years after his death, the Church ordered all his books burned, his bones dug up and burned, and his ashes scattered on the Thames River.

## From the Sermon, "See, Watch, and Pray"

*First Christ bids three things to those that are in orders: first, he bids that we shall see, and then, that we shall watch, and thirdly, that we shall pray, to continue the first two. The first is needful for prelates; for just as the sense of sight of all the senses shows a man*

to be most watchful, so sight of God's law makes a man most watchful unto God. For this law is faith, that man should be most studious
in. Christ bids that man should see, not vanities of the world, nor the
unstable law of man, for both these sights harm men, but the law of
Christ that is the book of life, and God's word, Jesus Christ.

# John Huss

## (1369–1415)

John Huss was ordained to the priesthood of the Roman Catholic Church in 1401 after receiving the Bachelor's and Master's degrees at the University of Prague. He preached against the evils of the Church and gained popular acceptance. He was the confessor for the Queen of Bohemia. He was a powerful preacher of Roman doctrine until he translated some of the sermons of John Wycliffe into the Bohemian language. These sermons moved him to cry out for reform in the Church and a return to the authority of the Scriptures as the sole source of faith and doctrine for the believer. Huss maintained that Christ, not Peter, was the foundation of the Church and that some Popes had been heretics. At once Huss was branded a heretic, excommunicated, and his writings were suppressed. He found refuge outside Prague, where he continued to preach, write and study. The chief product of Wycliffe's pen, *Concerning the Church*, developed his teachings concerning the universal priesthood of all believers, emphasizing that Christ is the only Head of the Church. Because of this, some credit Huss with beginning the reformation that Martin Luther carried to full bloom one hundred years later. In 1414, Huss was promised safe conduct by the Pope and Emperor Sigismund to the Council of Constance to present his views. Instead of hearing Huss, the Council had him arrested, gave him a mock trial without the benefit of an advocate, and condemned him to death as a heretic. He was kept in prison for seven months before he was burned. As Huss stood before the stake he said, "In the truth of the gospel which I have written, taught, and preached, I die willingly and joyfully today." Then the fire was kindled, and as the red tongues of flame driven by the wind from Lake Boden rose high around the body of the martyr, Huss sang, "Jesus Christ, the Son of the Living God, have mercy on me." The Pope dismissed his own broken promise of safe conduct to Huss with, "When dealing with heretics, one is not obligated to keep his word." The martyrdom of Huss kept the "religious pot" boiling for a hundred years so that a century later Martin Luther was warned against going to Leipzig even when promised a safe conduct by the Pope. The influence of Huss lived on through his preaching and the godly example of his death.

# Girolamo Savonarola

## (1452–1498)

Savonarola achieved a passion for study early in life due to his grandfather's influence. It was hoped that he would someday become a great physician. Religious feelings took possession of his soul. In 1474 a sermon preached by an Augustinian friar made such an impression on him that he formed an irrevocable decision to devote himself to the monastic life. He remained in a Dominican monastery for seven years.

Savonarola began to preach the Bible in Florence, Italy, in 1481, during the time of Lorenzo the Magnificent, when immorality, pleasure and ribald songs were prevalent and encouraged among the people of Florence. Savonarola in his first Lenten course at San Lorenzo in 1483 attracted few hearers, but two years later in a sermon on the Apocalypse, at Brescia, he made an indelible impression on his contemporaries by his threats of wrath to come as well as by the tender pathos of his assurance of the divine mercy for the penitent.

His fame as a preacher preceded him to Florence in 1491, and his ascendency over Florence began. Lorenzo tried in vain to silence the stern preacher or to induce him to moderate his violent denunciations, but to no avail. "Tell your master," he said to the messengers whom Lorenzo sent to him, "that albeit I am a humble stranger and he the lord of Florence, yet I shall remain and he shall depart." Lorenzo died the next year.

The city became a "republic" as a result of Savonarola's preaching. Because of his immense popularity with the common people, Savonarola was elected city manager.

Savonarola's preaching became increasingly vehement, and he proclaimed God's mercy on the good, His vengeance on the guilty. He saw, as he thought, the sword bent towards the earth: "the sky darkened, thunder pealed, lightning flashed, and the whole world was wasted by famine, bloodshed, and pestilence."

The appearance of the streets of Florence became completely changed. Hymns and chants replaced low songs; men and women dressed more conservatively and rejected worldly vanities. People of all sorts — nobles, scholars, artists — became monks. The city was transformed into a Christian republic, owning Christ as its Head.

Pope Alexander VI offered him a cardinal's position if he would quit preaching the Bible and exposing the sins of the Vatican. Savonarola refused the "red hat" of the cardinal and replied, "No hat will I have but that of a martyr reddened with my own blood."

He was excommunicated, imprisoned, tortured, and then burned at the stake. The morning he was led to the scaffold the Bishop pronounced the sentence, "I separate thee from the Church militant and the Church triumphant." Savonarola answered, "Not from the Church triumphant, that is beyond thy power." Before dying he said, "Rome will not quench this fire . . ."

## From the Sermon, "Penance"

*Your sins, then, O Italy, O Rome, O Florence, your impieties, your fornications, your cruelties, your sins, I say, beget these tribulations. Here is the cause! And if you have found the cause of all this evil, look for its remedy. Eradicate the sin that is the source of it, and you will be healed*: quia remota causa, removetur effectus. Take away the sins, and the tribulations will not harm you; *and if you do not do this,*

33

## Girolamo Savonarola

*believe me, nothing else will avail. You are deceiving yourselves, Italy and Florence, if you do not believe what I tell you. Nothing except penance will help you: do as you wish, but all will be in vain without it. You shall see.*

*O rich, O poor, do penance; and you rich, give alms to the poor. Peccata tua elemosinis redime. O you who fear God, do good and do not be afraid of tribulations, for God will give you great consolation in them. Penance is the only remedy; and if only you will truly repent, you will remove a great part of the tribulations. Agite poenitentiam, and remove the sins that are the cause of the tribulations.*

*And now, O priests, I must come back to you; I mean the bad ones, for I am always reverent to the good ones. Renounce, I say, that unspeakable vice, renounce that accursed vice that has so greatly provoked the wrath of God upon you. If you do not, woe, woe to you! O lustful ones, dress yourselves in hair-cloth and do that penance which you need! O you who have your houses full of vanities and pictures and indecent things and evil books, and that Morgante of yours and other poetry contrary to the faith, bring them to me to make a bon-fire or a sacrifice to God. And you, mothers, who adorn your daughters with so much vanity and extravagance and fancy hair ornaments, bring all these things here to us to throw into the fire, so that, when the wrath of God comes, He will not find them in your houses. And thus, I command you as your father. Now, if you will do thus in these matters, as I have told you, you will be sufficient, you alone, to placate the wrath of God; otherwise, I should regret to have to bring you bad tidings. . . .*

34

# Balthasar Hübmaier

## (1480–1528)

Hübmaier was born of poor parents in Augsburg, Germany. Although little is known of his early life, he was an unusual student, receiving the Master's degree in 1511 from the University of Freiburg and the Doctor of Theology degree two years later from the University of Ingolstadt, where he became professor of theology. Hübmaier was a student of Eck, the infamous Roman Catholic theologian, who debated Martin Luther in Leipzig. Soon Hübmaier's fame as a pulpit orator grew, and he was called to Regensburg as chief pastor in the cathedral. During these years a great change in his religious convictions took place as the result of his study of the Scriptures. There is no record of the date of his conversion; however, in the year 1522 he began to openly preach that the Roman Catholic Church had departed from the doctrines and practices of the Scriptures. He carried into the Reformation many from the parish in Waldshut. Hübmaier made a trip to Switzerland where he visited Erasmus and Zwingli, and soon thereafter he embraced Protestant theology. He rejected infant baptism and on Easter, 1525, he was baptized and he immediately immersed about three hundred followers. He also administered the Lord's Supper to his followers, even though the Catholic Church kept the cup from the laity. He traveled over Central and Western Europe and was continually in danger from the various religious and political authorities who constantly sought to arrest him. In 1526 he fled to Moravia, and as the result of his ministry in his new home, six thousand converts were baptized in one year. He was the author of many articles and pamphlets condemning and criticizing Rome. In 1528 authorities arrested him in Vienna, condemned him as a heretic, and on March 10 burned him at the stake. His faithful wife, who encouraged him to remain true to the Word of God, was drowned in the Danube River eight days later. He was faithful to the end and his influence continued in the lives of those he reached through his preaching and godly example.

# Martin Luther

## (1483–1546)

The great German Reformer, Martin Luther, was born November 10, 1483, in Eisleben, Saxony, and died there February 18, 1546. He was the second son of Hans Luther, a miner of Thuringian peasant stock. Martin studied at the University of Erfurt and received his Master of Arts degree in 1505. Following his father's desire, he began pursuing the law profession. However, traveling on foot from Mansfeld to Erfurt, he was surprised by a lightning bolt which struck him to the ground. He cried out, "St. Anna, help me, and I will become a monk." Luther later regretted the oath but felt bound to it. He entered the monastic order and became extremely ascetic to gain proper relationship with God.

In 1507, Luther was ordained a priest and began his work as a theological teacher, rising in academic rank. In 1508 he became a teacher at the University of Wittenberg. Luther obtained a doctorate of theology on October 19, 1512, and shortly thereafter became Staupitz' successor on the theological faculty as professor of Biblical theology.

Luther was plagued with an inner demand for true righteousness, something he could not attain through penance, monasticism, or the sacraments. Exegeting a passage in Romans (1:17), he discovered what he regarded as the true meaning of the Gospel. This permeated his teachings, and he became increasingly critical of Catholic theology, based on Aristotelian principles. In 1515 Luther became the priest of the City Church of Wittenberg. After much prayer, he tacked to the door of the Schlosskirche (Castle Church) in Wittenberg the ninety-five academic theses "on the power of indulgences." The point of these theses (the archbishop had given ninety-four commending indulgences) was that if indulgences were payments to be received as "good works" as a release from the temporal punishments of God, from the pains of purgatory, or from guilt, they were contrary to Christianity, which allows the believer to practice repentance throughout his whole life. Controversy developed, and he was denounced in Rome. Johann Eck became his chief opponent and charged Luther with heretical hostility to the Pope.

Luther defended himself brilliantly at a disputation at the general chapter of the Saxon Augustinians in Heidelberg, April 26, 1518.

Through the influence of Archduke Frederick and the University of Wittenberg, Luther's case was brought before Cardinal Cajetan at Augsburg instead of in Rome. Cajetan, angered that Luther would not recant, sought his arrest as a heretic. Cajetan claimed the Pope's permission, which he did not have. Political conditions kept the warrant from being issued, and Frederick protected Luther.

In 1520 Luther published a number of works which explained his position and built his popularity among theologians, clergymen, humanists, and the common people. Three of these are: *Open Letter to the Christian Nobility of the German Nation Concerning the Reform of the Christian Estate; On the Babylonian Captivity of the Church;* and *On Christian Liberty.* On December 10, 1520, Luther dramatically severed himself from obedience to the Pope by publicly burning a copy of the papal bulletin.

Luther was summoned to appear before the German Congress at Worms in 1521 to answer charges of heresy. Using the witness stand as a pulpit, Luther made his well-known defense. It is said (though possibly an interpolation) that he dramatically concluded with, "Here I stand! I cannot do otherwise! God help me!" He was promptly excommunicated from the Catholic Church.

Luther was safely conducted by friends to Wartburg Castle so that the Edict of Worms (a death warrant) was never executed.

Luther compiled a *Small Catechism* and a *Large Catechism* in 1529. These summarize his interpretation of the Christian Gospel and communicated the characteristic features of his faith to numerous generations of Lutherans. His commentaries on Galatians and Genesis became famous. His main work was furthering the Reformation, and he spent some twenty years translating the New Testament into German.

His last years were filled with pain resulting from digestive trouble. Luther had an extremely productive mind. He firmly established in Europe the three great truths of the New Testament which had been buried for centuries under ritual and dead formality: (1) Man is justified by faith alone. (2) Every believer is a priest with direct access to God through the Lord Jesus Christ. (3) The Bible apart from tradition is the sole source of faith and authority for the Christian.

# Martin Luther

## From the Sermon,
## "Justification by Faith"

*The foundation must be maintained without wavering, that faith
without any works, without any merit, reconciles man to God and
makes him good, as Paul says to the Romans: "But now apart from
the law a righteousness of God hath been manifested, being witnessed
by the law and the prophets; even the righteousness of God through
faith in Jesus Christ unto all them that believe." Paul at another
place says: "To Abraham, his faith was reckoned for righteousness"; so also with us. Again: "Being therefore justified by faith, we
have peace with God through our Lord Jesus Christ." Again: "For
with the heart man believeth unto righteousness; and with the mouth
confession is made unto salvation." These, and many more similar
passages, we must firmly hold and trust in them immovably, so that to
faith alone without any assistance of works, is attributed the forgiveness of sins and our justification.*

*Therefore the powerful conclusion follows, there must be some-
thing far greater and more precious than all good works, by which
a man becomes pious and good, before he does good; just as he must
first be in bodily health before he can labor and do hard work. This
great and precious something is the noble Word of God, which offers us in the Gospel the grace of God in Christ. He who hears and
believes this, thereby becomes good and righteous. Wherefore it is
called the Word of Life, a Word of Grace, a Word of Forgiveness.
But he who neither hears nor believes it, can in no way become good.
For St. Peter says in the Acts: "And he made no distinction between
us and them, cleansing their hearts by faith." For as the Word is, so
will the heart be, which believes and cleaves firmly to it. The
Word is a living, righteous, truthful, pure and good Word, so also
the heart which cleaves to it, must be living, just, truthful, pure and
good.*

*But true faith, of which we speak, cannot be manufactured by our
own thoughts, for it is solely a work of God in us, without any assistance on our part. As Paul says to the Romans, it is God's gift and
grace, obtained by one man, Christ. Therefore, faith is something
very powerful, active, restless, effective, which at once renews a person and again regenerates him, and leads him altogether into a new
manner and character of life, so that it is impossible not to do good
without ceasing.*

# Ulrich Zwingli

## (1484–1531)

Ulrich Zwingli was educated at schools in Basel and Bern, Switzerland, and Vienna, Austria. He had a happy boyhood with no great sense of sin. He became a parish priest in the Roman Catholic Church with little moral earnestness. On becoming pastor of the "Great Minster Church" in Zurich, Zwingli saw himself in the role of an Old Testament prophet and began to preach against the unscriptural practices in the Catholic Church. He made an open break with Rome in 1522 after studying the works of Martin Luther. The break was completed in 1525 when he replaced the Roman Mass with the first Reformed Communion service at his church. Later he removed images, relics and organs from the church and centered the service around the sermon. Zwingli differed with Luther in his views on Communion, maintaining that the Lord's Supper is only a memorial ordinance. The civil government supported Zwingli. The Reformation spread throughout Swiss centers because of his influence. Zwingli participated in armed warfare against the Catholic states around him and died in battle, sword in hand, defending the Bible over tradition.

## From Zwingli's Comments on Communion

*A sacrament is the sign of a holy thing. When I say: The sacrament of the Lord's body, I am simply referring to that bread which is the symbol of the body of Christ who was put to death for our sakes. The papists all know perfectly well that the word sacrament means a sign and nothing more, for this is the sense in which it has always been used by Christian doctors. Yet they have still allowed the common people to be deceived into thinking that it is something strange and unusual, something which they cannot understand and which for that reason they have come to equate with God himself, something which they regard as holy in that sense. But the very body of Christ is the body which is seated at the right hand of God, and the sacrament of his body is the bread, and the sacrament of his blood is the wine, of which we partake with thanksgiving. Now the sign and the thing signified cannot be one and the same. Therefore the sacrament of the body of Christ cannot be the body itself.*

42

# Menno Simons

## (1492–1559)

Menno Simons was born in Friesland, Holland. Little is known of his early life and education. In 1524 he was ordained to the priesthood of the Roman Church; however, his study of the New Testament produced doubts concerning many of the Roman doctrines. Luther's writings influenced him to leave the Roman Church. Simons' preaching thereafter is described as evangelical rather than sacramental. Simons went farther than either Luther or Calvin in rejecting the teachings of Romanism and he identified himself with the Dutch Anabaptists. He was baptized in 1537 by Obbe Philip. His fame as a writer and as a preacher grew, and soon the Anabaptists of that area acknowledged him as their leader. In his church discipline, which was drawn from the Swiss Baptists, silent prayer was common, and sermons were without texts. He taught that neither Baptism nor Communion conferred grace upon an individual, but that grace was obtained only through faith in the Lord Jesus Christ. His preaching and influence were such that many of the Dutch Anabaptists adopted his name and thereafter were known as Mennonites.

## From Simons' Book,
### *Foundation of Christian Doctrine*

*In the third place we teach with Christ and say, Believe the Gospel. That Gospel is the blessed announcement of the favor and grace of God to us, and of forgiveness of sins through Christ Jesus. Faith accepts this Gospel through the Holy Ghost, and does not consider former righteousness or unrighteousness, but hopes against hope (Rom. 4:18), and with the whole heart casts itself upon the grace, Word and promises of the Lord, since it knows that God is true, and that His promises cannot fail. In this the heart is renewed, converted, justified, becomes pious, peaceable, and joyous, is born a child of God, approaches with full confidence the throne of grace, and so becomes a joint heir of Christ and a possessor of eternal life.*

*Such persons awaken in time. They hear and believe the Word of the Lord. They weep over their past vain lives and conduct. They desire help and aid for their sick souls. To such, Christ who is a comforter for all troubled hearts says, Believe the Gospel, that is, fear not; rejoice and be comforted; I will not punish nor chastise you, but will heal you, comfort you, and give you life. A bruised reed will I not break, and smoking flax will I not quench. I will seek that which was lost and bring back again that which was driven away and will bind up that which was broken and will strengthen that which was sick. I am not come to call the righteous, but sinners to repentance. By the kindness of my heavenly Father, I am come into the world, and by the power of the Holy Ghost, I became a visible, tangible, and dying man; in all points like unto you, sin excepted. I was born of Mary, the unpolluted mother and pure virgin; I descended from heaven, sprang from the mouth of the Most High, the firstborn of every creature, the first and last, the beginning and the end, the Son of the Almighty God; anointed with the Holy Ghost to preach the Gospel to the poor, to bind up the brokenhearted, to proclaim liberty to the captives, to give sight to the blind, to open the prison to them that are bound, and to proclaim the acceptable year of the Lord. Believe the Gospel. I am the Lamb that was sacrificed for you all. I take away the sins of the whole world. My Father has made me unto you wisdom, righteousness, sanctification, and redemption. Whosoever believeth on me shall not be ashamed; yea, all that believe that I am He, shall have eternal life.*

# William Tyndale

## (1494–1536)

Bible translator and reformer, Tyndale was ordained as a priest in 1521, having studied Greek diligently at Oxford and Cambridge universities. Following his studies he joined Sir John Walsh's household, with duties not easy to define. Some accounts describe him as a tutor to Sir John's children; some make him chaplain to the household; while another suggests he acted as secretary to Sir John. One day Tyndale was engaged in a discussion with a learned man who told him it was better to be without God's law than that of the Pope. To this Tyndale retorted that he defied the Pope and all his laws, adding that if God were to spare his life, before many years passed he would cause a boy who drove the plough to know more of the Scriptures than this learned man. Tyndale had found his vocation — translation of the Bible into English.

Tyndale conferred with Luther in Germany and stayed on the continent translating the Bible from Greek into English. The printing of the translation was begun at Cologne in 1525, but was stopped by an injunction obtained by Johann Dobeneck, a vain and conceited man who hated the Reformation and opposed it in every possible way. Tyndale fled to Worms, where the book was printed. Copies were smuggled into England, where Archbishop Warham and Bishop Tonstall ordered them seized and burned.

Eventually Tyndale was betrayed by a friend and arrested in Brussels, Belgium. Despite the efforts of Thomas Cromwell and others to save him, he was tried for treason and heresy against the Church. He was condemned, degraded from holy orders, strangled, and his body burned. His last words were a prayer, "Lord, open the king of England's eyes."

Tyndale's influence upon English literature was great, chiefly through the use made of his renderings in the King James Version of the Bible (1611). It is estimated that 60 percent of this translation is derived from that of Tyndale.

# PART IV

# THE CHURCH EXPANDS

## A.D. 1500 to The Present

Christianity was confronted with several forces as it entered this period. There was the passing of the Medieval culture with which Christianity had been identified. The rise of nationalism in Europe affected religious life. As the monarchs of these states struggled with each other for supremacy, they also sought to control the church in order to make Christianity an instrument of the state. This period was also characterized by scientific advance. Many of those who led this scientific advance began to question the relevance and reasonableness of Christianity. This was also the period of territorial expansion across the Atlantic and of the rise of the middle class.

This period opened with more threats and challenges to a divided and corrupt Christianity. The Papacy was decadent. All the historic sights of Christianity except Rome — Jerusalem, Antioch, Alexandria, and Constantinople — were under Moslem rule, and Western Europe appeared to be outgrowing Christianity.

Yet within the church, movements and individuals brought about new life and vitality, resulting in a complete separation from the Roman Catholic Church. Martin Luther, John Calvin, and Ulrich Zwingli led in the Reformation. These Protestants repudiated the authority of the Pope. They stressed the authority of the Bible and faith as the only means of salvation. In the meantime the Roman Catholic Church purified itself of much corruption and by the middle of the seventeenth century it had won back some of the territory lost to Protestantism.

However, in the latter part of the eighteenth century a combination of movements and events dealt severe blows to Christianity and caused another recession. There was a growing de-Christianization of large segments of "Christian" Europe. Yet there were renewals of true Christian life among these peoples. The climate of opinion favored Deism, which ruled out some of the historic theological features of Christianity. A Christ-denying romanticism was also making headway. The political revolutions such as that in France were spearheaded by Deism and seemed to be the wave of the future. Just as these influences were triumphing, Christianity was once again showing signs of life which were to break forth shortly.

In Europe, after 1815, Christianity was characterized by a vitality that spread through many men and movements. It inspired many men to rethink their faith in terms of the age in which they lived. It transformed millions of lives and gave birth to societies which spread the Gospel to all the continents and many of the islands. This was the period of the separation of church and state. Germany took the leading position in the field of theology and Bible study.

There was an immense growth of Christianity in Great Britain during the years 1815–1900, primarily through the Sunday school. With it came a high peak of foreign missionary service. As they built their world empire, the British mission societies spread Christianity throughout the world. During these years nonconformist religious groups grew and separated from the established church. With their growth, there was a parallel growth of evangelicalism. These groups spurred an evangelical revival across the British Isles and a missionary effort throughout the world. The vitality of Christianity brought about social change. However, on the Continent, liberalism (theological modernism) was beginning to spread.

As a result of these developments in Europe and Britain, as well as in the United States, Christianity made inroads in North Africa, Western Asia, and Eastern Europe. Christianity became the dominant religion in the Pacific, especially in Australia and New Zealand. During this century, Christianity became stronger in South Africa and South and East Asia than it had ever been.

Much of the immigration to the United States during these years was Protestant. In the United States Christianity won over many of those who tended toward de-Christianization. Protestantism made advances among non-Christian groups such as the Indians, Negroes and Orientals. This advance was spurred on by the revivalism of the years 1815–1900. Christianity was characterized by the rise and arrival of many denominations. It had profound effects on society, for example, the end of Negro slavery and educational advance.

Nineteenth century Christianity became more widely spread geographically than any other faith had ever been, and it exercised an extensive influence as missionaries spread the faith through the Plains States of the United States and into foreign countries. The logical application and outworking of Biblical principles produced much social change wherever Christianity took hold. Education was expanded, hospitals were founded, the status of women was raised, slavery was abolished. It also brought on prison reform, better care for the insane, and legislation to protect children and women workers, shorten work hours, safeguard workers' health, and improve their housing. It established colleges and universities, and later Bible schools. Christianity influenced literature and philosophy and molded the thinking of statesmen such as Lincoln and Gladstone, and eventually molded some laws of these nations. Perhaps most important, millions of individual lives were transformed by God's power.

51

# John Calvin

## (1509–1564)

John Calvin became a leading force in furthering the Reformation movement in France. He was born in Noyon, Picardy, and died in Geneva, Switzerland. Calvin was the fourth son of Gerard Cauvin, notary and secretary to the chapter of Noyon Cathedral. Calvin's father provided his son with a good education, having him tutored in the house of Adrien de Hangest; later he attended the College des Capettes, a boys' school in Noyon. Cauvin wanted his brilliant son to enter the priesthood and sent him to the University of Paris (1523). The next move for Calvin was to the more celebrated College de Monteigne, but the environment was decidedly worse. Noel Beda, who had condemned Luther two years earlier, taught theology. Here Calvin learned logic from Beda but didn't appear to be influenced by Beda's theology. Early in 1528 Calvin received the Master of Arts degree. Calvin's father felt law would be a more profitable pursuit, so at eighteen Calvin obeyed and attended the University of Orleans. He began learning Greek under Melchior Wolmar, a German of Lutheran inclination.

Calvin had a "sudden conversion" and wrote in the introduction to his *Commentary on the Psalms* concerning this experience, "Since I was more stubbornly addicted to the superstitions of the papacy than to be easily drawn out of so deep a ruine, God subdued my heart — too stubborn for my age — to docility by a sudden conversion."

Planning to go to Strasbourg and continue writing, he was forced to detour through Geneva because of the war between Francis I and Charles V. Against his own preferences he was thrust into public leadership of the Reformation. The churches of the city were used for evangelistic preaching. Calvin began to lecture in the Cathedral of St. Pierre on the Epistles of St. Paul.

The chief governing body of the city, known as the Little Council, met with Calvin and decided to effect discipline. A document describing the short confession of faith and instruction formed characteristic features of later Calvinism. Resistance to the discipline caused Calvin to leave the city.

In 1541 the city of Geneva invited Calvin back, and he remained until he died. A system of discipline was outlined called the *Ecclesiastical Ordinances.* Calvin continually expanded the *Institutes of the Christian Religion,* which is the foundation for Calvinism. This work has become the basis for Presbyterian and Reformed church doctrine and practice. Geneva, in effect, had become the "Rome of Protestantism."

From
### *The Institutes of the Christian Religion*

*What is God? Men who pose this question are merely toying with idle speculations. It is far better for us to inquire, "What is his nature?" and to know what is consistent with his nature. What good is it to profess with Epicurus some sort of God who has cast aside the care of the world only to amuse himself in idleness? What help is it, in short, to know a God with whom we have nothing to do? Rather, our knowledge should serve first to teach us fear and reverence; secondly, with it as our guide and teacher, we should learn to seek every good from him, and, having received it, to credit it to his account. For how can the thought of God penetrate your mind without your realizing immediately that, since you are his handiwork, you have been made over and bound to his command by right of creation, that you owe your life to him? — that whatever you undertake, whatever you do, ought to be ascribed to him? If this be so, it now assuredly follows that your life is wickedly corrupt unless it be disposed to his service, seeing that his will ought for us to be the law by which we live. Again, you cannot behold him clearly unless you acknowledge him to be the fountainhead and source of every good. From this too would arise the desire to cleave to him and trust in him, but for the fact that man's depravity seduces his mind from rightly seeking him.*

*For, to begin with, the pious mind does not dream up for itself any god it pleases, but contemplates the one and only true God. And it does not attach to him whatever it pleases, but is content to hold*

53

*him to be as he manifests himself; furthermore, the mind always exercises the utmost diligence and care not to wander astray, or rashly and boldly to go beyond his will. It thus recognizes God because it knows that he governs all things; and trusts that he is guide and protector, therefore giving itself over completely to trust in him. Because it understands him to be the Author of every good, if anything oppresses, if anything is lacking, immediately it betakes itself to his protection, waiting for help from him. Because it is persuaded that he is good and merciful, it reposes in him with perfect trust, and doubts not that in his loving-kindness a remedy will be provided for all its ills. Because it acknowledges him as Lord and Father, the pious mind also deems it meet and right to observe his authority in all things, reverence his majesty, take care to advance his glory, and obey his commandments. Because it sees him to be a righteous judge, armed with severity to punish wickedness, it ever holds his judgment seat before its gaze, and through fear of him restrains itself from provoking his anger. And yet it is not so terrified by the awareness of his judgment as to wish to withdraw, even if some way of escape were open. But it embraces him no less as punisher of the wicked than as benefactor of the pious. For the pious mind realizes that the punishment of the impious and wicked and the reward of life eternal for the righteous equally pertain to God's glory. Besides, this mind restrains itself from sinning, not out of dread of punishment alone; but, because it loves and reveres God as Father, it worships and adores him as Lord. Even if there were no hell, it would still shudder at offending him alone.*

*Here indeed is pure and real religion: faith so joined with an earnest fear of God that this fear also embraces willing reverence, and carries with it such legitimate worship as is prescribed in the law. And we ought to note this fact even more diligently: all men have a vague general veneration for God, but very few really reverence him; and wherever there is great ostentation in ceremonies, sincerity of heart is rare indeed.*

# John Knox

## (1513–1572)

Born in Scotland, John Knox was ordained as a Catholic priest sometime between 1530 and 1540. He was converted to Christ after he met a Bible-believing Christian, George Wishart. Wishart was burned at the stake in 1546. Shortly afterwards Knox was arrested by the "authorities" and made a galley slave for nineteen months. He went to England in 1549 and preached the Bible until the reign of Bloody Mary, during which time he lived in Frankfort, Germany. There he came under the influence of Calvin. He returned to Scotland after several years in Geneva and began preaching against the papal church. He was arrested under Queen Mary Stuart in 1560 and tried for treason but acquitted.

One of the greatest contributions Knox made to the Reformation in Scotland was the *Book of Discipline,* which he and his associates prepared at the request of Parliament. The book was the brainchild of Knox. In it he set forth principles for the guidance of the Church. He gave a strong emphasis to the nature of education. He urged the nation to provide for the education of all children. Stalker wrote that nothing bears more distinctly the impress of Knox's genius as does the *Book of Discipline.* "It comes away in a single gush, and it causes a dazzling image of national prosperity to rise before the mind."

In the *Book of Discipline* Knox called for a system of education that was breathtaking for that age.

> Every town should have a schoolmaster, and in every rural parish the minister or reader should teach the children and come to them. Men should be compelled by the Kirk and the magistrates to send their children — bairns — to school. Poor men's children should be helped, and no one should be denied basic education.

In Knox's *History of the Reformation of Religion within the Realme of Scotland,* he wrote,

> The necessity of schools. Seeing that God hath determined that His church here on earth shall be taught not by angels but by men; and seeing that men are born ignorant of all godliness; and seeing, also, how God ceaseth to illumine to men miraculously, suddenly changing them, as He changed His apostles and others in the primitive Church; it is necessary that your honours of this realm, if ye now thirst unfeignedly for

the advancement of Christ's glory, or desire the continuance of His benefits to the generation following. For as the youth must succeed to us, so ought we to be careful that they have knowledge and erudition, for the profit and comfort of that which ought to be most dear to us, to wit, the church and Spouse of the Lord Jesus.

Knox spent his remaining years preaching and lecturing in Edinburgh and St. Andrews. Above all others he was the maker of Protestant Scotland. He preached "hell-fire and damnation" to Queen Mary of Scotland and also to Bloody Mary, Queen of England. Of him it was said, "Here is one who never feared the face of man."

## From the Sermon,
## "The Source and Bounds of Kingly Power"

*The prophet saith, "O Lord our God, other lords besides Thee have ruled us."*

*For the better understanding of this complaint, and of the mind of the prophet, we must, first, observe from whence all authority flows; and secondly, to what end powers are appointed by God: which two points being discussed, we shall better understand what lords and what authority rule beside God, and who they are in whom God and His merciful presence rules.*

*The first is resolved to us by the words of the Apostle, saying, "There is no power but of God." David brings in the eternal God speaking to judges and rulers, saying, "I have said, ye are gods, and sons of the Most High." From which place it is evident that it is neither birth, influence of stars, election of people, force of arms, nor, finally, whatsoever can be comprehended under the power of nature, that makes the distinction betwixt the superior power and the inferior, or that establishes the royal throne of kings; but it is the only and perfect ordinance of God, who willeth His terror, power, and majesty, partly to shine in the thrones of kings, and in the faces of judges, and that for the profit and comfort of man. So that whosoever would study to deface the order of government that God has established, and allowed by His holy word, and bring in such a confusion that no difference should be betwixt the upper powers and the subjects, does nothing but avert and turn upside down the very throne of God, which He wills to be fixed here upon earth; as in the end and cause of this ordinance more plainly shall appear: which is the second point we have to observe, for the better understanding of the prophet's words and mind.*

*The end and cause then, why God imprints in the weak and feeble flesh of man this image of His own power and majesty is not, to puff up flesh in opinion of itself; neither yet that the heart of him that is exalted above others should be lifted up by presumption and pride, and so despise others; but that he should consider he is appointed lieutenant to One, whose eyes continually watch upon him, to see and examine how he behaves himself in his office. St. Paul, in few words, declares the end wherefore the sword is committed to the powers, saying, "It is to the punishment of the wicked doers, and unto the praise of such as do well."*

*Of which words it is evident that the sword of God is not committed to the hand of man to use as it pleases him, but only to punish vice and maintain virtue, that men may live in such society as is acceptable before God. And this is the true and only cause why God has appointed powers in this earth.*

*The first thing then that God requries of him who is called to the honor of a king, is, The knowledge of His will revealed in His word.*

*The second is, An upright and willing mind, to put in execution such things as God commands in His law, without declining to the right, or to the left hand.*

*Kings, then, have not an absolute power to do in their government what pleases them, but their power is limited by God's word; so that if they strike where God has not commanded, they are but murderers; and if they spare where God has commanded to strike, they and their throne are criminal and guilty of the wickedness which abounds upon the face of the earth, for lack of punishment.*

*Wouldst thou, O Scotland! have a king to reign over thee in justice, equity, and mercy? Subject thou thyself to the Lord thy God, obey His commandments, and magnify thou the Word that calleth unto thee, "This is the way, walk in it;" and if thou wilt not, flatter not thyself; the same justice remains this day in God to punish thee, Scotland, and thee Edinburgh especially, which before punished the land of Judah and the city of Jerusalem.*

# Roger Williams

## (1603–1684)

Founder of the first Baptist church in America, Roger Williams was born in London and raised in the Episcopal Church, of which he was made a rector. Becoming dissatisfied with the ritual and ceremony of his church, he became a Puritan. He came to America and preached in Boston and Plymouth, Massachusetts, where he taught separation of church and state and complete religious freedom.

Williams created quite a commotion within a short time after his arrival and this is readily seen in an article of Cotton Mather's *Magnalia*:

> In the year 1654 a certain windmill in the Low countries, whirling around with extraordinary violence by reason of a violent storm then blowing; the stone at length by its rapid motion became so intensely hot as to fire the mill, from whence the flames, being dispersed by high winds, did set a whole town on fire. But I can tell my reader that, above twenty years before this, there was a whole country in America like to be set on fire by the rapid motion of a windmill in the head of one particular man.

The windmill in the head of Williams was nothing more than stubborn honesty and forthrightness of speech. He denounced the failure of the churches publicly to separate themselves from the false practices of the Church of England. In addition he attacked the charter of the colony on the ground that the king had no title to the land and that a valid title could be secured only from the Indians.

Williams was banished from Salem for his convictions and preaching, after which he went to Narragansett Bay, where he did missionary work among the Indians. It was there that he founded the settlement of Providence, Rhode Island, on land purchased from the Indians. At this time he became a Baptist and was immersed in water for the first time since his conversion. He served as governor of the colony from 1654 to 1657, but he practiced his separation of church and state doctrines even as a civic ruler. He was distinguished from other New Englanders by the singleness of devotion with which he pursued the implications of assumptions common to them all. The will of God must be done in spite of all earthly considerations.

## From a Letter to Major Mason

*How much sweeter is the counsel of the Son of God to mind first the matters of his Kingdom; to take no care for tomorrow; to pluck out, put off, and fling away right eyes, hands, and feet, rather than to be cast whole into hell-fire; to consider the ravens and the lilies,*

*whom a Heavenly Father so clothes and feeds; and the counsel of his servant Paul to roll our cares, for this life also, upon the Most High Lord, steward of his people, the eternal God: to be content with food and raiment; to mind not our own, but every man the things of another; yea and to suffer wrong, and part with what we judge is right, yea, our lives. . . . This is humanity. Yea, this is Christianity.*

# Richard Baxter

## (1615–1691)

Richard Baxter was born in Rowton, England. His parents were poor, his early education was limited. Later he attended school at Wroxeter and read with Richard Wickstead at Ludlow Castle. His eager mind found abundant nourishment in the large library of the castle. Later, he was persuaded to enter court life in London, but returned home to study theology. While reading theology with the local clergyman, he met Joseph Symonds and Walter Cradock, two famous nonconformists, whose piety and fervor influenced him considerably. In 1638 he was appointed master of the free grammar school, Dudley, in which place he commenced his ministry, having been ordained and licensed by John Thornborough, Bishop of Worcester. His early ministry was not successful, but during these years he took a special interest in the controversy relating to nonconformity and the Church of England. Rejecting episcopacy, he soon became alienated from the Church, and known as a moderate conformist. In April 1641 at twenty-six, he became pastor in the village of Kidderminster and remained there for nineteen years, accomplishing an unusual work of reformation in that place. His ministry was interrupted often by civil war. At one time he served as chaplain of the army. After the Restoration in 1660, Baxter went to London and ministered there as chaplain to King Charles II until Parliament passed the Act of Uniformity, which required all clergymen to agree to everything in the Anglican Book of Common Prayer. Baxter refused and lost his position as chaplain and Bishop of Hereford. In addition he was prohibited from preaching in his parish of Kidderminster, and from 1662 to 1687 he was continually persecuted. He retired to Acton in

Middlesex for the purpose of quiet study and writing. While there he was arrested and imprisoned for conducting a conventicle. His most memorable words at this time were: "I preached as never sure to preach again, and as a dying man to dying men." In 1685 he was accused of libeling the Church of England in one of his books. His trial is regarded by many historians as one of the most brutal perversions of English justice in history, and he was again imprisoned. During the years of oppression, his health grew worse, yet these were his most productive years as a writer. His books and articles flooded England. Finally in 1691 ill health, aggravated by eighteen years in prison, caused his death. He had preached before the king, the House of Commons, the Lord Mayor of London; his prolific pen had produced one hundred and sixty-eight theological and devotional works. His saintly behavior, great talents, wide influence, added to his extended age, had raised him to a position of unequalled reputation as the "English Demosthenes" in the conflict for liberty of conscience.

## From the Sermon,
## "Making Light of Christ and Salvation"

*O that I could make every man's conscience a preacher to himself that it might do it, which is ever with you! That the next time you go prayerless to bed, or about your business, conscience might cry out, Dost thou set no more by Christ and thy salvation? That the next time you are tempted to think hardly of a holy and diligent life (I*

## Richard Baxter

will not say to deride it as more ado than needs), conscience might cry out to thee, Dost thou set so light by Christ and thy salvation? That the next time you are ready to rush upon known sin, and to please your fleshly desires against the command of God, conscience might cry out, Is Christ and salvation no more worth than to cast them away, or venture them for thy lusts? That when you are following the world with your most eager desires, forgetting the world to come, and the change that is a little before you, conscience might cry out to you, Is Christ and salvation no more worth than so? That when you are next spending the Lord's day in idleness or vain sports, conscience might tell you what you are doing. In a word, that in all your neglects of duty, your sticking at the supposed labor or cost of a godly life, yea, in all your cold and lazy prayers and performances, conscience might tell you how unsuitable such endeavors are to the reward; and that Christ and salvation should not be so slighted. I will say no more but this at this time, It is a thousand pities that when God hath provided a Saviour for the world, and when Christ hath suffered so much for their sins, and made so full a satisfaction to justice, and purchased so glorious a kingdom for his saints, and all this is offered so freely to sinners, to lost, unworthy sinners, even for nothing, that yet so many millions should everlastingly perish because they make light of their Saviour and salvation, and prefer the vain world and their lusts before them. I have delivered my message, the Lord open your hearts to receive it. I have persuaded you with the word of truth and soberness; the Lord persuade you more effectually, or else all this is lost. Amen.

# George Fox

## (1624–1691)

The founder of the Society of Friends (Quakers), Fox was born at Drayton-In-The-Clay, Leicestershire, England, of Puritan parents.

His formal education was slight, and as a child he was quite responsive to spiritual teaching and of serious disposition. He wrote in his *Journal* concerning his early years:

> In my very young years I had a gravity and stayedness of mind and spirit not usual in young children: insomuch that when I saw old men behave lightly and wantonly toward each other, I had a dislike thereof raise in my heart, and I said within myself, "If ever I come to be a man, surely I shall not do so, nor be wanton."

He was converted at age nineteen after leaving home and wandering around the countryside. At last he found himself brought "by the power of Christ" through this "ocean of darkness and death" into the revelation of God's love. In 1649 he was imprisoned for interrupting a preacher and again in 1650 for alleged blasphemy. Fox was persecuted almost daily in his itinerant ministry, yet his power of endurance was phenomenal. He was beaten with dogwhips, knocked down with fists and stones, brutally struck with pike staves, threatened by mobs, imprisoned eight times in filthy prisons and dungeons: yet he went straight forward with his mission. He attempted to let the new life in Christ take its own free course.

During 1651 his itinerant preaching resulted in many converts. In 1652 he convinced some hundreds at meetings in Westmoorland, and the Society of Friends was born. For the rest of his life Fox traveled continually throughout England, and to Wales, Scotland, Ireland, the Netherlands, Germany, the West Indies, and North America.

Through his combination of tenderness and gentleness, Fox was able to attract a large body of people from various classes, including William Penn and Robert Barclay, who not only shared his principles but were devoted to him personally. Through his organizing ability and the establishment in 1667 of a system of monthly business meetings (still in use), a certain stability accompanied Quakerism in its early years.

William Penn had described him as "an original, being no man's copy," and "as ready to forgive as unapt to take or give an offence." Fox died in London on January 13, 1691, and was buried in the Friends' burial ground near Bunhill Fields.

His life demonstrated the truth of his famous saying, "One man raised by God's power to stand and live in the same spirit as the apostles and prophets can shake the country for ten miles around."

# John Bunyan

## (1628–1688)

John Bunyan, called the "Shakespeare among divines," was born in Elstow, England, near Bedford, where he spent most of his life. Although today he is regarded as a literary genius, he had little formal education. At the age of sixteen, this rough and profane young man enlisted in the army of Parliament and saw active duty during the English civil war. In 1647, at the age of nineteen, he married a young woman who persuaded him to attend church with her regularly. Here he heard the Gospel, and after a deep and prolonged soul struggle he made a complete surrender to Christ, after which he was baptized and joined the Baptist church of Bedford. Soon he began to preach in the church and in the surrounding villages. The people recognized in Bunyan the elements of leadership as well as an ability to expound the Scriptures. Continuing in his trade as a tinker, he witnessed wherever he went. He spent his holidays and Sundays preaching in barns, shops, village greens, as well as in the open air, where he attracted great crowds. He was arrested and imprisoned in 1660 for conducting a conventicle, a religious meeting without the permission of the state church. When offered his freedom if he would promise not to preach, he refused and was jailed. While imprisoned he studied, wrote, and supported his family by making and selling shoe laces. It was while a prisoner that he wrote his immortal *Pilgrim's Progress*. In 1672 he was released and immediately resumed his ministry. During the last sixteen years of his life he was active as pastor, writer, counselor, administrator, and pastor-in-chief to a multitude of churches and young ministers. Bunyan was a champion for the cause of religious liberty and freedom of conscience in spiritual matters. One who knew him wrote: "The grace of God was magnified in him and by him and a rich anointing of the spirit was upon him; and yet this great saint was always in his own eyes the chiefest of sinners and the poorest of saints." He died in 1688 after riding forty miles in a driving rain on horseback to London to preach. He was always a poor man, yet through his example, his ministry, and especially his pen, he left invaluable riches to posterity.

## From *Pilgrim's Progress*

Then said Evangelist, "If this be thy condition, why standest thou still?" He answered, "Because I know not whither to go." Then he gave him a parchment roll, and there was written within, "Fly from the wrath to come."

The man therefore read it, and, looking upon Evangelist very carefully, said, "Whither must I fly?" Then said Evangelist pointing

with his finger over a very wide field, "Do you see yonder wicket gate?" The man said, "No." Then said the other, "Do you see yonder shining light?" He said, "I think I do." Then said Evangelist, "Keep that light in your eye, and go up directly thereto; so shalt thou see the gate; at which, when thou knockest, it shall be told thee what thou shalt do."

# Jonathan Edwards

## (1703–1758)

Especially known as a leader of the Great Awakening, Edwards was born in East Windsor, Connecticut, October 5, 1703. His father was minister there for sixty years.

Jonathan was the only son among ten daughters. The whole family was well educated and they helped Jonathan to gain remarkable intellectual facility at an early age. When ten years old he wrote a semi-humorous tract on the immateriality of the soul. He entered Yale College in 1716 at only thirteen years of age. He struggled with God's absolute sovereignty, considering it a horrible doctrine until his last year of college when it came to be for him, "exceedingly pleasant, bright and sweet." His conversion followed shortly after graduation.

He was ordained in February 1727 at Northampton, becoming an assistant to his grandfather, Solomon Stoddard. He spent thirteen hours a day studying. Sarah Pierpont, age seventeen, became his bride that same year. She was the daughter of James Pierpont, a founder of Yale and a great granddaughter of Thomas Hooker.

In 1729 Stoddard died, leaving Jonathan with sole charge of one of the largest and wealthiest congregations in the colony. Edwards delivered a lecture two years later entitled, *God Glorified in the Word of Redemption by the Greatness of Man's Dependence Upon Him in the Whole of It,* which was published with a preface by two Boston ministers. It was the start of a lifelong fight against eighteenth-century rationalism in New England theology. He attacked Arminianism, and while yet a student compiled two collections of his writings: *Notes on Natural Science* and *Notes on the Mind,* both concerned with Calvinism and man's volition.

Edwards viewed the pastor as one who should act as a prophet by expounding the laws of God to the unlearned. He resolved not to make it appear "as if I was much read, or was conversant with books, or with the learned world." His preaching technique was as unemotional as possible. Putting little fervor into his messages, he would use vivid, common illustrations to forcefully convey Scriptural teaching. The sermon, *Sinners in the Hands of an Angry God* states, "The God that holds you over the pit of hell, much as one holds a spider, or some loathsome insect, over the fire, abhors you, and is dreadfully provoked."

Edwards' first great revival began in 1734 at Northampton. He himself wrote an account of this revival, "A Faithful Narrative of the Surprizing Work of God" (1736), which was published in England and on the continent. In 1740 the colonies were engulfed in the Great Awakening revivalistic fervor of the great preacher, George Whitefield.

Because of Edwards' viewpoint on membership in the church, and also the backwash of the revival, the church at Northampton deposed him. He delivered his *Farewell Sermon* on June 22, 1750. He then became a missionary to the remnants of the Mohican Indians living near Stockbridge, Massachusetts, and pastor of the village church. He developed the works which brought him recognition as a metaphysician and theologian. In 1758 he was invited to be president of the College of New Jersey (now Princeton University). Immediately afterwards he died from a smallpox vaccination.

The revival of his day ran from 1734 to 1744. Through Edwards' preaching thousands were converted to the Lord Jesus Christ.

## From the Sermon,
## "Sinners in the Hands of an Angry God"

*There are, in the souls of wicked men those hellish principles reigning, that would presently kindle and flame out in hell-fire, if it were not for God's restraints. There is laid in the very nature of carnal men, a foundation for the torments of hell: there are those corrupt principles, in reigning power in them, and in full possession of them, that are the beginnings of hell-fire.*

*So that thus it is, that natural men are held in the hand of God*

# Jonathan Edwards

*over the pit of hell; they have deserved the fiery pit, and are already sentenced to it; and God is dreadfully provoked, His anger is as great toward them as to those that are actually suffering the executions of the fierceness of His wrath in hell, and they have done nothing in the least to appease or abate that anger, neither is God in the least bound by any promise to hold them up one moment; the devil is waiting for them, hell is gaping for them, the flames gather and flash about them, and would fain lay hold on them and swallow them up; the fire pent up in their own hearts is struggling to break out; and they have no interest in any Mediator, there are no means within reach that can be any security to them. In short, they have no refuge, nothing to take hold of; all that preserves them every moment is the mere arbitrary will, and uncovenanted, unobliged forbearance of an incensed God.*

*The use may be of awakening to unconverted persons in this congregation. This that you have heard is the case of every one of you that are out of Christ. That world of misery, that lake of burning brimstone, is extended abroad under you. There is the dreadful pit of the glowing flames of the wrath of God; there is hell's wide gaping mouth open; and you have nothing to stand upon, nor any thing to take hold of. There is nothing between you and hell but the air; it is only the power and mere pleasure of God that holds you up.*

*O sinner! consider the fearful danger you are in: it is a great furnace of wrath, a wide and bottomless pit, full of the fire of wrath that you are held over in the hands of that God whose wrath is provoked and incensed as much against you as against many of the damned in hell; you hang by a slender thread, with the flames of Divine wrath flashing about it, and ready every moment to singe it, and burn it asunder; and you have no interest in any mediator, and nothing to lay hold of to save yourself, nothing to keep off the flames of wrath, nothing of your own, nothing that you have ever done, nothing that you can do to induce God to spare you one moment.*

# John Wesley

## (1703–1791)

John Wesley, founder of the Methodist movement, was born in 1703 at Epworth, England, where his father, the Reverend Samuel Wesley, was rector. John's mother, Susanna, was most influential in shaping the lives of her children. She gave each of the children one hour per week on a fixed day for religious conversation and prayer. John was so apt a learner that his father thought him fit for partaking of Communion at a very early age. This religious training accounts for much of his later work among children.

Wesley entered Oxford in 1720, receiving a Master of Arts degree in 1727. At that time he was not yet converted to Christ, although he endeavored to lead a clean, moral life and pursue the subject of religion. *Faith*, during this period, seems to have meant little more than "right opinion."

Wesley was ordained a deacon in September 1725 and preached his first sermon at South Leigh, a small village near Witney. In March 1726, he was elected Fellow of Lincoln College. During this time he became a religious devotee and determined to give all his energy to the ministry.

Commenting on his preaching activity following his first four years at Oxford, Wesley says,

> From the year 1725 to 1729 I preached much, but saw no fruit of my labour. Indeed it could not be that I should; for I neither laid the foundation of repentance nor of preaching the Gospel, taking it for granted that all to whom I preached were believers, and that many of them needed no repentance. From the year 1729 to 1734, laying a deeper foundation of repentance, I saw a little fruit. But it was only a little — and no wonder: for I did not preach faith in the blood of the covenant.

During John's absence from college in 1727, his brother Charles (four years younger) had become serious in seeking God, along with a few undergraduates. The group came to be known as the Holy Club and later as the Methodists, because of their methodical habits. Upon John's return, he was made the head of this company. Their activities included visiting prisoners, instructing ignorant children, relieving the poor, fasting and holding Communion on a weekly schedule. Among the early members was George Whitefield, who later continued John's work in Georgia and was influential in the Great Awakening revival movement in America.

In 1735 John, along with his brother Charles, journeyed to the colony of Georgia as a missionary of the Propagation Society. Moravian missionaries in Georgia, with whom Wesley had contact aboard ship, were influential in his later conversion to Christ. He had never appropriated Christ as his personal Saviour but had been a High Anglican churchman, rigidly adhering to ritual and law with a tingling mixture of mysticism. John Wesley left Georgia a failure in his ministry to the colonists and Indians.

On May 14, 1738, at a meeting of a religious society in Aldersgate Street, London, Wesley testified that, "I felt my heart strangely warmed. . . ." The following spring after hearing the account of Jonathan Edwards' success in New England and of George Whitefield's successes at outdoor preaching, Wesley obtained his first significant results. The Methodist Revival was launched, and he remained at its head for more than fifty years. He spent the rest of his life preaching in the fields, the streets, and in the Methodist preaching chapels. He was up each morning before five o'clock for prayer and Bible study, and rode on horseback fifteen to twenty miles a day, preaching four or five times daily. During his lifetime Wesley traveled two hundred and fifty thousand miles preaching a total of forty-two thousand sermons. His activities and administrations are recorded in his *Journal* and letters. He died at the age of eighty-eight and preached up to the very month of his death.

## From the *Journal of John Wesley*

### Jan. 24, 1738

*I went to America, to convert the Indians; but oh, who shall convert me? who, what is he that will deliver me from this evil heart of unbelief? I have a fair summer religion. I can talk well; nay, and believe myself, while no danger is near. But let death look me in the face, and my spirit is troubled. Nor can I say, 'To die is gain'!*

> I have a sin of fear, that when I've spun
> My last thread, I shall perish on the shore!

*I think, verily, if the gospel be true, I am safe: for I not only have given, and do give, all my goods to feed the poor; I not only give my body to be burned, drowned, or whatever God shall appoint for me; but I follow after charity (though not as I ought, yet as I can), if haply I may attain it. I now believe the gospel is true. "I show my faith by my works," by staking my all upon it. I would do so again and again a thousand times, if the choice were still to make. Whoever sees me, sees I would be a Christian. Therefore "are my ways not like other men's ways." Therefore I have been, I am, I am content to be, "a by-word, a proverb of reproach." But in a storm I think, What if the gospel be not true? Then thou art of all men most foolish. For what hast thou given thy goods, thy ease, thy friends, thy reputation, thy country, thy life? For what art thou wandering over the face of the earth? — A dream, a cunningly-devised fable! Oh, who will deliver me from this fear of death? What shall I do? Where shall I fly from it? Should I fight against it by thinking or by not thinking of it? A wise man advised me some time since, "Be still, and go on." Perhaps this is best, to look upon it as my cross; when it comes, to let it humble me, and quicken all my good resolutions, especially that of praying without ceasing; and at other times, to take no thought about it, but quietly to go on "in the work of the Lord."*
*May 14, 1738*

*In the evening I went very unwillingly to a society in Aldersgate Street, where one was reading Luther's preface to the Epistle to the Romans. About a quarter before nine, while he was describing the change which God works in the heart through faith in Christ, I felt my heart strangely warmed. I felt I did trust in Christ, Christ alone for salvation; and an assurance was given me that He had taken away my sins, even mine, and saved me from the law of sin and death.*

# George Whitefield
## (1714–1770)

One of the most influential preachers of all time, George White-field, the English evangelist, was born in Gloucester, England. He was the son of a saloon operator. His father died two years after George's birth, and his mother kept the tavern to support the seven small children. George was a real "scamp," owing to his environmental upbringing. However, he did develop a love for reading and acting plays that contributed to his later success as a great orator. He desired to attend Oxford and did so, working his way through by waiting on tables. Prior to his conversion Whitefield had several times expressed his desire to become a clergyman. He attempted to please God through his efforts, but would alternate between spells of "saint" and "sinner." He met the Wesleys, and they became close friends. Because this was previous to John's own conversion, what they had to offer was strict legalism. He would deny himself all physical comfort by fasting and refusing to do things he enjoyed. After one period of fasting, he physically collapsed, and it was during his recovery that the way of salvation became clear to him. He experienced what he characterized as "joy unspeakable and full of glory."

Whitefield was ordained a deacon in 1736 and began to preach in jails. Later he did missionary work in the colony of Georgia. He made seven trips to America, where he played an important role in the Great Awakening.

During the early stages of his ministry he was popular, but after arriving back in Great Britain and preaching quite strongly against the drinking and frivolities of that day, he found it increasingly difficult to obtain a pulpit in the established church. This resulted in his turning to the "open-air" meetings which became his trademark. He preached wherever crowds gathered, even at dances and races. The people flocked to hear him. Although he condemned their practices, thousands were converted to Christ. Benjamin Franklin was puzzled over the fact that so many came when they were so plainly condemned for their wickedness.

Whitefield operated the first orphanage in the United States,

Bethesda, in Georgia. He appealed to crowds on both sides of the Atlantic for its support. Franklin wanted it to be relocated in Philadelphia, and when Whitefield refused, he resolved not to support the work. However, his resolution was not fulfilled as he describes it,

> I had in my pocket a handful of copper money, three or four silver dollars, and five pistoles in gold. As he proceeded I began to soften and concluded to give the copper. Another stroke of his oratory determined me to give the silver; and he finished so admirably that I emptied my pocket wholly into the collection dish, gold and all!

In 1741 the breach between John Wesley and Whitefield occurred. Whitefield was Calvinist, and Wesley was Arminian. They were reconciled before Whitefield's death, and Wesley preached a noble memorial sermon for his friend.

His speaking often had remarkable effects upon his audiences. On one occasion, referred to as the *Cambuslang Revival,* he preached at noon, again at six, and again at nine. At eleven there was a commotion. Conviction seized the sinners, some began weeping. Soon thousands wept, and at times their wails would drown the voice of the preacher. It is said that his voice could be heard for a mile without amplification.

David Hume, the great scientist and philosopher who was not particularly noted for "friendliness" toward evangelical preachers, declared that he would go twenty miles to hear Whitefield. He was indeed a "mighty voice" for thirty-four years of ministry, averaging ten sermons a week. His printed sermons produce some disappointment, being detached from the man. On a balcony not far from his deathbed, he preached his last message to more than two thousand people and died within an hour after extending the invitation to the lost to repent and receive Christ.

## From the Sermon, "The Method of Grace"

*The prophet gives a thundering message, that they might be terri-*

*fied and have some convictions and inclinations to repent; but it seems that the false prophets, the false priests, went about stifling people's convictions, and when they were hurt or a little terrified, they were for daubing over the wound, telling them that Jeremiah was but an enthusiastic preacher, that there could be no such thing as war among them, and saying to people, Peace, peace, be still, when the prophet told them there was no peace. The words, then, refer primarily unto outward things but I verily believe have also a further reference to the soul, and are to be referred to those false teachers, who when people were under conviction of sin, when people were beginning to look towards heaven, were for stifling their convictions and telling them they were good enough before. And, indeed, people generally love to have it so; our hearts are exceedingly deceitful, and desperately wicked; none but the eternal God knows how treacherous they are.*

*We are all desirous of peace; peace is an unspeakable blessing; how can we live without peace? And, therefore, people from time to time must be taught how far they must go, and what must be wrought in them, before they can speak peace to their hearts. This is what I design at present, that I may deliver my soul, that I may be free from the blood of all those to whom I preach — that I may not fail to declare the whole counsel of God. I shall, from the words of the text, endeavor to show you what you must undergo, and what must be wrought in you before you can speak peace to your hearts.*

*There is a great multitude of souls here; how shortly must you all die, and go to judgment! Even before night, or tomorrow's night, some of you may be laid out for this kirk-yard. And how will you do if you be not at peace with God — if the Lord Jesus Christ has not spoken peace to your heart? If God speak not peace to you here, you will be damned forever. I must not flatter you, my dear friends, I will deal sincerely with your souls. Some of you may think I carry things too far. But, indeed, when you come to judgment, you will find what I say is true.*

# David Brainerd

## (1718–1747)

David Brainerd was born April 20, 1718, at Haddam, Connecticut. His father died when David was nine and his mother died five years later. Early in life, Brainerd felt the call to the ministry and looked forward almost impatiently to the day when he could preach the Gospel. His formal education consisted of three years at Yale, after which ill health forced him to return home. He was an excellent student. He completed his studies privately until he was licensed by the association of ministers in Fairfield County, Connecticut, to preach. He turned down the offers of two pastorates in order to preach the Gospel to the American Indians.

Brainerd did his greatest work by prayer. He was alone in the depths of the forests unable to speak the language of the Indians, but he spent whole days in prayer. Once he preached through a drunken interpreter, a man so intoxicated he could hardly stand, yet scores were converted through that sermon. Plagued by ill health and the hardships of the primitive conditions, he died at the early age of twenty-nine at the home of Jonathan Edwards, to whose daughter he was engaged. After his death, William Carey read his diary and went to India; Robert McCheyne read it and went to the Jews; Henry Martyn read it and went to India. Though it was not written for publication, his diary influenced hundreds to yearn for the deeper life of prayer and communion with God, and also moved scores of men to dedicate themselves to missionary work.

## From His Diary on an Occasion in Which the Indians Were About to Engage in Idolatrous Feast and Dance

*In prayer I was exceedingly enlarged, and my soul was drawn out as ever I remember it to have been in my life. I was in such anguish, and pleaded with such earnestness that when I rose from my knees I could scarcely walk straight. The sweat ran down my face and body. I was wholly free from selfish ends in my supplications for the poor Indians. I knew they were met together to worship devils and not God, and this made me cry earnestly that God would appear and help me in my attempts to break up this idolatrous meeting.*

*Thus I spent the evening, praying incessantly for divine assistance and that I might not be self-dependent. What I passed through was remarkable, and there appeared to be nothing of any importance to me but holiness of heart and life, and the conversion of the heathen to God. All my cares, fears and desires disappeared, and were of little more importance than a puff of wind. I longed that God would*

get to Himself a name among the heathen, and I appealed to Him
with the greatest freedom that He knew I "preferred Him above my
chief joy."

Indeed, I cared not where or how I lived, or what hardships I went
through so that I could but gain souls to Christ. I continued in this
frame all evening and night. While I was asleep, I dreamed of these
things, and when I waked, the first thing I thought of was this
great work of pleading for God against Satan.

# John Newton

## (1725–1807)

John Newton was the son of an English sea captain. His mother, a deeply pious woman, gave him spiritual instruction until she died when John was seven years old. At the age of eleven John went to sea and spent the next twenty years as a sailor engaged in slave trading. His life was spent in the lowest sort of wickedness. At one time he himself was the property of an African woman who fed him only that which she threw under her table. He was nearly killed several times during terrible storms at sea. During one of these storms his wicked life passed before him, and deep conviction caused him to cry out to God for salvation. The next several years were spent in preparation for the ministry. He learned Latin, Greek, and Hebrew, and studied the Scriptures intensively. In 1764 he was appointed pastor in the parish of Olney, England, where he served for sixteen years before moving to St. Mary Woolnoth in the city of London. In addition to his pastoral duties, Newton was an ardent writer. His works included *Omicron, Narrative, Review of Ecclesiastical History,* and *Cardiphonia.* His greatest fame came from his work as a writer of hymns, the most familiar being "Amazing Grace" which depicts in its verses the life story of John Newton.

### Amazing Grace

*Amazing Grace! How sweet the sound, that saved a wretch like me!*
*I once was lost but now am found; was blind but now I see.*

*'Twas grace that taught my heart to fear, and grace my fears relieved;*
*How precious did that grace appear the hour I first believed;*

*Through many dangers, toils and snares, I have already come;*
*'Tis grace hath brought me safe thus far, and grace will lead me home.*

*The Lord has promised good to me, His word my hope secures;*
*He will my shield and portion be as long as life endures.*

*When we've been there ten thousand years, bright shining as the sun,*
*We've no less days to sing God's praise than when we first begun.*

# Francis Asbury

## (1745–1816)

The "Father of American Methodism" was born near Birmingham, England. His parents were poor, and Francis was apprenticed to a maker of "buckle chapes" after a short period of schooling. This hard work provided a better foundation than a great education, when one considers the work Francis was to do in America. Francis' parents were probably converts under the Wesleys, and Francis accepted Christ at thirteen. He soon became active in the ministry and at sixteen became a local preacher. In 1767 John Wesley recognized his ability and made him an itinerant minister. John Wesley spoke at the annual conference in 1771 and remarked, "Our brethren in America call aloud for help," and then he inquired (perhaps rhetorically), "Who will go?" Immediately a young man of twenty-six sprang to his feet. The following year, Asbury was appointed by Wesley as "general assistant" in charge of the work in America.

During the Revolutionary War, the Methodists were suspected of Loyalism, principally because they refused to take the prescribed oath; and many of their ministers returned to England. Asbury remained and continued his itinerant preaching. He eventually was driven to exile in Delaware, where he remained quietly, though not idle, for two years.

In 1784 Wesley appointed Asbury and Rev. Thomas Coke as superintendents or "bishops" of the church of the United States. Asbury refused to accept the position until it was ratified by the conference, since Wesley acted before such a conference decision was made. From this conference dates the actual beginning of the "Methodist Episcopal Church of the U.S.A."

To appreciate Francis Asbury one must examine his tremendous vitality, dedication and executive ability. He preached wherever people congregated: behind the barracks, from a wagon, from a window, upon the banks of a river, in a paper mill, in a tobacco house, and in an orchard. Once at Tarborough he found a fire in the hearth of a small apartment above the courthouse. Supposing it to be for preaching he soon discovered it was for a dance instead. The dancing was soon stopped, and Asbury had a "serious congregation to hear."

He led in establishing new settlements on the frontier. Annually he

# Francis Asbury

rode six thousand miles and preached from three to five hundred sermons. His last entry in his journal reads, "My consolations are great. I live in God from moment to moment."

## From *Journal and Letters of Francis Asbury*
*July 1815*

*I have frequently skimmed along the frontiers, for four and five hundred miles, from Kentucky to Greenbrier, on the very edge of the wilderness; and thence along Tigers Valley to Clarksburgh on the Ohio. These places, if not the haunts of savage men, yet abound with wild beasts. I am only known by name to many of our people, and some of our local preachers; and unless the people were all together, they could not tell what I have had to cope with. I make no doubt the Methodists are, and will be, a numerous and wealthy people, and their preachers who follow us will not know our struggles but by comparing the present improved state of the country with what it was in our days, as exhibited in my Journal and other records of that day.*

# William Carey

## (1761–1834)

William Carey, known as the "Father of Modern Missions," was born in Northamptonshire, England. Carey showed a great desire for learning early in life, but due to the poverty of the family, he had to work as a shoemaker's assistant. Carey did not mind the work, and to his joy he had the opportunity to learn several languages through acquiring books on the subjects and through private tutoring by friends. He mastered Dutch, French, Greek, Latin, and Hebrew before he was twenty years of age. Two years later he joined the Baptist Church and began preaching immediately, mostly on the theme of foreign missions. Carey desired to see his denomination engage in missionary activity.

Once at a ministerial meeting held at Northampton, he proposed mission work among the heathen. He was promptly told, "Sit down, young man, when God sees fit to convert the heathen, He will do so of His own accord."

Carey continued to cherish the dream of missions and wrote a treatise entitled, "An Inquiry on Missions." This was published and formed the basis for his great sermon on Christ's mission work, which he delivered on May 31, 1792, in Nottingham. This laid the foundation for Baptist mission work in India. Choosing Isaiah 54:2, 3 as his text for this occasion, Carey emphasized two lessons from it, that Christians expect great things of God and that they attempt great things for God.

He helped organize the English Baptist Missionary Society and was one of its first missionaries to India. In spite of several obstacles including scorn for being a cobbler, Carey made the voyage. His services were remarkable for their range and depth.

Carey translated the Bible into forty-four languages and dialects. In addition to soul-winning, Carey founded the Serampore College. He was also instrumental in developing grammars and dictionaries in Bengali, Sanskrit, and other native tongues.

## From Carey's introduction to
### An Enquiry Into the Obligation of Christians to Use Means for the Conversion of the Heathen

*As our blessed Lord has required us to pray that his will be done on earth as it is in heaven, it becomes us not only to express our desires of that event by words, but to use every lawful method to spread the knowledge of his name. In order to do this, it is necessary that we should become, in some measure acquainted with the religious state of the world; and as this is an object we should be prompted to pursue not only by the gospel of our Redeemer, but*

*even by the feelings of humanity, so an inclination to conscientious activity therein would form one of the strongest proofs that we are the subjects of grace, and partakers of that spirit of universal benevolence and genuine philanthropy, which appear so eminent in the character of God himself.*

# Christmas Evans

## (1766–1838)

Christmas Evans was born near the village of Llandyssul, Cardigan-shire, on Christmas Day, 1766. His father, a shoemaker, died soon after, and Christmas grew up as an illiterate farm laborer in the care of a godless, cruel uncle. At the age of seventeen, he became a ser-vant to a Presbyterian minister in whose church he was converted dur-ing a revival meeting. He learned to read and write and then took such an interest in spiritual things that his former companions in sin beat him severely, putting out one of his eyes. The Baptists of Llandyssul influenced him greatly, and he joined the Baptist Church. The warm acceptance of Christian hospitality left a lifelong impact on this young lad.

In 1790 at the age of twenty-four, Evans was ordained and be-gan to travel the entire country of Wales, preaching in churches, coal mines, and fields. The forgiveness of sin and grace of God were constant themes in his preaching. A remarkable manifestation of the Holy Spirit accompanied his ministry, and revival swept the country. Thousands were converted, and many thousands of Christians began to openly witness for Christ and sing hymns publicly as testimony of their salvation. Called the "Welch revival," the fame of the spiritual renewal spread around the world. A newspaper man reported that the grace of God visited men and women at various places in the country, usually without a human preacher, convicting of sin and moving people to seek repentance – a visitation from heaven. Those in the church attributed the revival to Evans – both his preaching and his praying. In spite of his early disadvantages and personal dis-figurement, Christmas Evans was a remarkably powerful preacher. He united a nimble mind and an inquiring spirit with his super-natural calling from God. Evans' character was simple, his piety gen-uine, and his faith fervently evangelical. His chief characteristic was a vivid and affluent imagination, which under the control of the Holy Spirit, earned for him the name of "The Bunyan of Wales."

# Peter Cartwright

## (1785–1872)

Peter Cartwright was born in Amherst County, Virginia. His father was a colonial soldier in the War of Independence. Shortly after the war, the family moved to Kentucky. Peter Cartwright was reared in frontier surroundings, and like many of the young men in that primitive area, engaged in sinful practices. His mother, a devout Christian woman, opened their cabin home for preaching by the Methodist circuit preachers. As a young man of sixteen, Peter was convicted of his sins as a result of these meetings, and after several weeks of deep agony and contrition, he was "soundly converted" at an outdoor revival meeting. His new faith completely changed his life, and Cartwright immediately began to witness for Christ. One year later he was licensed as an "exhorter" and began riding a circuit of his own. His appointments were few and far between, and he preached wherever people would open their homes, because "meeting houses" were few. This was the beginning of his long career as a circuit-riding Methodist preacher. Cartwright was a "hellfire and brimstone" preacher after the style of Wesley, and his character and personality often matched his sermons. Often he personally thrashed the "rowdies" who disturbed his camp meetings, after which he saw many of them "get religion." His fearlessness is described in an incident which took place in Nashville. As he was preaching, General Andrew Jackson entered the service. The local preacher whispered the news to Cartwright which prompted him to thunder, "And who is General Jackson? If General Jackson doesn't get his soul converted, God will damn him as quickly as anyone else." Jackson smiled and later told Cartwright that he was a "man after my own heart." In over fifty years of traveling circuits in Kentucky, Tennessee, Ohio, Indiana and Illinois, Cartwright received ten thousand members into the Methodist Church, personally baptized twelve thousand people, and preached more than fifteen thousand sermons. He was strongly opposed to easy religion, education and culture in the ministry. His equipment consisted of a black broadcloth suit and a horse with saddlebags, while his library was composed of a Bible, a hymnbook, and a copy of *Methodist Discipline*. He was the epitomy of the Methodist circuit riders who firmly planted the "old time religion" in the frontier of the infant United States of America.

## From the *Autobiography of Peter Cartwright*

. . . they cursed me, and told me to mind my own business, and said they would not get down. I stopped trying to preach, and called for a magistrate. There were two at hand, but I saw they were both afraid. I ordered them to take these men into custody, but they said they could not do it. I told them, as I left the stand, to command me to take them, and I would do it at the risk of my life. I advanced toward them. They ordered me to stand off, but I advanced. One of them made a pass at my head with his whip, but I closed in with him, and jerked him off the seat. A regular scuffle ensued. The congregation by this time were all in commotion. I heard the magistrates give general orders, commanding all friends of order to aid in suppressing the riot. In the scuffle I threw my prisoner down, and held him fast; he tried his best to get loose; I told him to be quiet, or I would pound his chest well. The mob rose, and rushed to the rescue of the two prisoners, for they had taken the other young man also. An old and drunken magistrate came up to me, and ordered me to let my prisoner go. I told him I should not. He swore if I did not, he would knock me down. I told him to crack away. Then one of my friends, at my request, took hold of my prisoner, and the drunken justice made a pass at me; but I parried the stroke, and seized him by the collar and the hair of the head, and fetching him a sudden jerk forward, brought him to the ground, and jumped on him. I told him to be quiet, or I would pound him well. The mob then rushed to the scene; they knocked down seven magistrates, and several preachers and others. I gave up my drunken prisoner to another, and threw myself in front of the friends of order. Just at this moment the ringleader of the mob and I met; he made three passes at me, intending to knock me down. The last time he struck at me, by

95

# Peter Cartwright

*the force of his own effort he threw the side of his face toward me. It seemed at that moment I had not power to resist temptation, and I struck a sudden blow in the burr of the ear and dropped him to the earth. Just at that moment the friends of order rushed by hundreds on the mob, knocking them down in every direction. In a few minutes, the place became too strait for the mob, and they wheeled and fled in every direction; but we secured about thirty prisoners, marched them off to a vacant tent, and put them under guard till Monday morning, when they were tried, and every man was fined to the utmost limits of the law. The aggregate amount of fines and costs was near three hundred dollars. They fined my old drunken magistrate twenty dollars, and returned him to court, and he was cashiered of his office. On Sunday, when we had vanquished the mob, the whole encampment was filled with mourning; and although there was no attempt to resume preaching till evening, yet, such was our confused state, that there was not then a single preacher on the ground willing to preach, from the presiding elder, John Sale, down. Seeing we had fallen on evil times, my spirit was stirred within me. I said to the elder, "I feel a clear conscience, for under the necessity of the circumstances we have done right, and now I ask to let me preach."*

*"Do," said the elder, "for there is no other man on the ground can do it."*

*My text was, "The gates of hell shall not prevail." In about thirty minutes the power of God fell on the congregation in such a manner as is seldom seen; the people fell in every direction, right and left, front and rear. It was supposed that not less than three hundred fell like dead men in mighty battle; and there was no need of calling mourners, for they were strewed all over the camp-ground; loud wailings went up to heaven from sinners for mercy, and a general shout from Christians, so that the noise was heard afar off. Our meeting lasted all night, and Monday and Monday night; and when we closed on Tuesday, there were two hundred who had professed religion, and about that number joined the Church.*

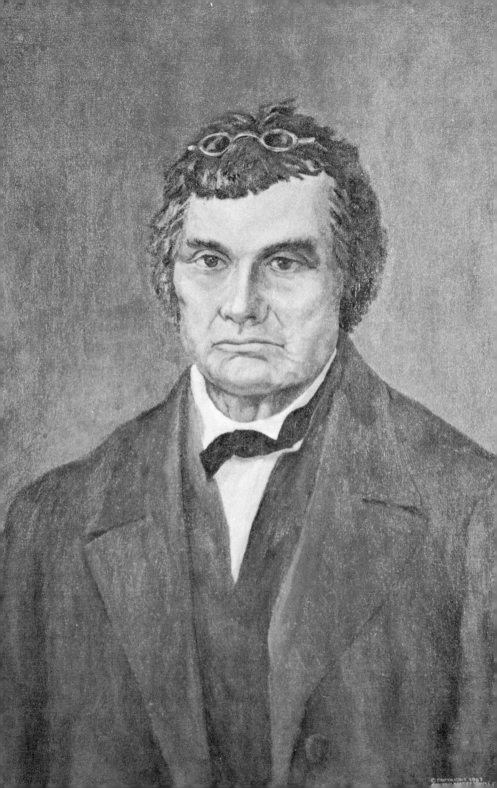

# Adoniram Judson

## (1788–1850)

Adoniram Judson, the son of a Congregational minister, learned to
read at the age of three and by his tenth year knew Latin and Greek.
A serious student of theology, Judson entered Brown University at the
age of sixteen and graduated three years later as the valedictorian of
his class. At Andover Theological Seminary he could not get away
from the words of a missionary appeal, "Go ye into all the world."
This occurred after hearing a sermon entitled, "The Star in the East,"
which had as a text Matthew 2:2. The leading thought of the sermon
was the evidence of the Divine power of the Christian religion in the
East. In a letter written many years afterward, he says:

> Though I do not now consider that sermon as peculiarly ex-
> cellent, it produced a very powerful effect on my mind. For
> some days I was unable to attend to the studies of my class,
> and spent my time in wondering at my past stupidity, depicting
> the most romantic scenes in missionary life, and roving about
> the college rooms declaiming on the subject of missions. My
> views were very incorrect, and my feelings extravagant; but yet
> I have always felt thankful to God for bringing me into that
> state of excitement, which was perhaps necessary, in the first
> instance, to enable me to break the strong attachment I felt to
> home and country, and to endure the thought of abandoning
> all my wanted pursuits and animating prospects. That excite-
> ment soon passed away; but it left a strong desire to prosecute
> my inquiries and ascertain the path of duty. It was during a
> solitary walk in the woods behind the college, while meditating
> and praying on the subject, and feeling half inclined to give up,
> that the command of Christ, 'Go into all the world and preach
> the Gospel to every creature,' was presented to my mind with
> such clearness and power, that I came to a full decision, and
> though great difficulties appeared in my way, resolved to obey
> the command at all events.

In 1810 Judson helped form the American Board of Commissioners for Foreign Missions, and two years later he and his new wife, Ann, sailed for India. When they were refused entrance, they went to Burma, where they worked for six years before winning the first convert to Christ. During those years they were plagued with ill health, loneliness, and the death of their baby son. Judson was imprisoned for nearly two years, during which time Ann faithfully visited him, smuggling to him food, books, papers, and notes which he used in translating the Bible into the Burmese language. Soon after his release, Ann and their baby daughter, Maria, died of spotted fever. Judson withdrew into seclusion into the interior of Burma where he completed the translation of the whole Bible into Burmese. In 1845 he returned to America, but the burning desire to win the Burmese people sent him back to the Orient, where he soon died. As a young man he had cried out, "I will not leave Burma until the cross is planted here forever." Thirty years after his death, Burma had sixty-three Christian churches, one hundred and sixty-three missionaries, and over seven thousand baptized converts.

### Judson Longing for His Burman Home

A stranger in my native land!
　　O home beyond the sea,
How yearns with all its constant love,
　　This weary heart for thee.

I left thee, when around my hearth
　　Was gathering thickest gloom,
And gentle ones have since that hour
　　Descended to the tomb.

99

## Adoniram Judson

A flower has withered on thy breast,
    Thou wilt that treasure keep;
And sweet her rest, whose grave is made
    Away upon the deep.

I once trod lightly on the turf
    That I am treading now;
The flush of hope was on my cheek,
    And youth was on my brow —

But time hath wrought a wondrous change
    In all I loved — and *me!*
I prize thee, native land — but more,
    My home beyond the sea.

O Burmah! shrouded in the pall
    Of error's dreadful night!
For wings — for wings once more to bear
    To thy dark shores the light:

To rear upon thy templed hills,
    And by thy sunny streams,
The standard of the Cross, where now
    The proud Pagoda gleams.

One prayer, my God! Thy will be done —
    One only boon I crave:
To finish well my work, — and rest
    Within a Burman grave!

# Charles Grandison Finney

## (1792–1875)

The United States' "new measure" evangelist was born in Warren, Connecticut, and grew up in Oneida County, New York. He taught school for a few years and studied law privately. In 1818 he entered the law office of Benjamin Wright in Adams, New York.

While reading Blackstone's *Commentaries on Law*, he noted continuous reference to the Mosaic institutions. Blackstone repeatedly mentioned the Bible as the highest authority. Finney soon bought a Bible and was reading it more than law. The Word of God brought deep conviction to his soul, and on October 10, 1821, out in the woods, he was converted to Christ. With his conversion he became convinced that he had been given a "retainer from the Lord Jesus Christ to plead His cause," so he dropped his law practice to become an evangelist, and within two years he was licensed by the Presbyterians.

Finney's methods involved using features of frontier revivals and addressing the people as he would a jury. These methods, after being carried into the larger cities, were labeled as "new measures." He received much opposition from the trained ministers from the New England schools. However, he managed to polish his methods somewhat and was exceedingly successful in the larger cities.

The highlight of his evangelistic ministry was the "nine mighty years" of 1824-1832, during which he conducted powerful revival meetings all over the eastern cities of Gouverneur, Rome, Utica, Auburn, Troy, Wilmington, Philadelphia, Boston and New York. During his meetings in Rochester, New York, it is reported, "the place was shaken to its foundations"; twelve hundred people united with the churches of Rochester Presbytery; all the leading lawyers, physicians, and businessmen were saved; forty of the converts entered the ministry; and the whole character of the town was changed. As a result of that meeting, revivals broke out in fifteen hundred other towns and villages.

In 1832 he began an almost continual revival in New York City as the pastor of the Second Free Presbyterian Church. He didn't completely agree with the Presbyterian polity, and his supporters built the Broadway Tabernacle for him in 1834. Two years later he withdrew from the Presbytery, and the church became Congregational in polity. In 1835 he became professor of theology at Oberlin College, Ohio, dividing his time between the school and his New York tabernacle. In 1837 he broke with the Broadway Tabernacle to become minister of the First Congregational Church in Oberlin. From 1851 to 1866 he also served as president of the college. He died August 16, 1875.

Over five hundred thousand people responded to his public invitations to receive Christ. Finney was personal, home-spun, dramatic, and forceful, and his revival lectures are still studied by Bible-believing preachers, teachers, and evangelists.

## From Finney's *Autobiography*

*Just at this point the whole question of gospel salvation opened to my mind in a manner most marvelous to me at the time. I think I then saw, as clearly as I ever have in my life, the reality and fullness of the atonement of Christ. I saw that His work was a finished work: and that instead of having, or needing, any righteousness of my own to recommend me to God, I had to submit myself to the righteousness of God through Christ. Gospel salvation seemed to me to be an offer of something to be accepted; and that it was full and complete; and that all that was necessary on my part, was to get my own consent to give up my sins, and accept Christ. Salvation, it seemed to me, instead of being a thing to be wrought out, by my own works, was a thing to be found entirely in the Lord Jesus Christ, who presented himself before me as my God and my Saviour.*

*Without being distinctly aware of it, I had stopped in the street right where an inward voice seemed to arrest me. How long I remained in that position I cannot say. But after this distinct revelation had stood for some little time before my mind, the question seemed to be put, "Will you accept it now, today?" I replied, "Yes, I will accept it today, or I will die in the attempt."*

*Just at this moment I again thought I heard some one approach*

103

*me, and I opened my eyes to see whether it was so. But right there the revelation of my pride of heart, as the great difficulty that stood in the way, was distinctly shown to me. An overwhelming sense of my wickedness in being ashamed to have a human being see me on my knees before God, took such powerful possession of me, that I cried at the top of my voice, and exclaimed that I would not leave that place if all the men on earth and all the devils in hell surrounded me. "What," I said, "such a degraded sinner as I am, on my knees endeavoring to make my peace with my offended God!" The sin appeared awful, infinite. It broke me down before the Lord.*

*I told the Lord that I should take him at his word; that he could not lie; and that therefore I was sure that he heard my prayer, and that he would save me. He then gave me many other promises, both from the Old and the New Testament, especially some most precious promises respecting our Lord Jesus Christ. I never can, in words, make any human being understand how precious and true those promises appeared to me. I took them one after the other as infallible truth, the assertions of God who could not lie. They did not seem so much to fall into my intellect as into my heart, to be put within the grasp of the voluntary powers of my mind; and I seized hold of them, appropriated them, and fastened upon them with the grasp of a drowning man.*

*But how was I to account for the quiet of my mind? I tried to recall my convictions, to get back again the load of sin under which I had been laboring. But all sense of sin, all consciousness of present sin or guilt, had departed from me. I was so quiet and peaceful that I tried to feel concerned about that, lest it should be a result of my having grieved the Spirit away.*

*The repose of my mind was unspeakable. I never can describe it in words. The thought of God was sweet to my mind, and the most profound spiritual tranquility had taken full possession of me. This was a great mystery; but it did not distress or perplex me . . . I just accepted it.*

# Robert Moffat

## (1795–1883)

Robert Moffat was born in Ormiston, Scotland, of pious but poor parents. At a young age he became an apprentice to learn gardening. Upon the completion of this apprenticeship, he moved to England, where he was led to Christ through the efforts of the Wesleyan Methodists. Already having an intense desire to serve the Lord, Moffat attended a missionary conference held in Manchester, where he felt the divine call to carry the Gospel to the heathen. He was later accepted by the London Missionary Society, and at the age of twenty-one sailed for Cape Town, South Africa. The hardships and primitive conditions did not deter him as he pushed northward into the interior, where he led to Christ the most dangerous outlaw chief in that region. Returning to Cape Town in 1819, he met his fiance arriving from England, and they were married. Together they spent the next fifty-one years on the mission field experiencing many hardships and sorrows of that primitive area. Three of their children died in infancy and youth; however, five remained in Africa as missionaries. Mary, the oldest daughter, became the wife of David Livingstone. The work of Moffat was, as it were, the stepping stone which others used in spreading the Gospel throughout the dark continent. He opened many mission stations and served as a pioneer missionary in an area of hundreds of square miles. He translated the Bible into the language of the Bechwanas after reducing the language to written characters. In 1870 after fifty-four years in Africa, he and his wife returned to England, where she died one year later. Moffat continued to promote foreign missions the rest of his life. He raised funds for a seminary at the Kuruman Station, where native students were prepared for missionary work among their own people. At his death in 1883, the London newspapers said: "Perhaps no more genuine soul ever breathed . . . he addressed the cultured audiences within the majestic halls of Westminster Abbey with the same simple manner in which he led the worship in the huts of the savages."

# George Müller

## (1805–1898)

George Müller was born and raised in Prussia, and lived in sin and crime even while studying for the ministry of the state church. He was converted at a prayer meeting in a private home, and from that time his life was changed. Müller moved to England and there sought acceptance by the London Missionary Society as a missionary to the Orient. After his rejection he began preaching and ministering wherever the door was opened. His preaching led him to Bristol, where in 1834 he founded the Scriptural Knowledge Institution for Home and Abroad. One year later he opened his first orphans' home for twenty-six girls, even though he had no financial assistance. By 1870 he had built five large orphans' homes and was feeding 2,100 orphans daily. He solicited no financial help and told only the Lord of the daily needs. Only born-again Christians were accepted for service in the institutions. Many children were won to Christ each year. The Scriptural Knowledge Institution also was instrumental in sending missionaries, Bibles, and Gospel literature around the world. The various schools operated by the institution matriculated over 121,000 students, with thousands of them receiving Christ while in the schools. The institution distributed almost three hundred thousand Bibles in different languages in addition to one and one-half million New Testaments. One hundred and sixty-three missionaries were sent out and/or supported, and over 111 million tracts distributed. In all, in a period of sixty-three years God poured out in response to the faith and prayers of George Müller over seven and one-half million dollars for the spreading of the Gospel. Müller read the Bible through over two hundred times, half of that on his knees, where he claimed the promise, "Open wide thy mouth and I will fill it." He spent his last seventeen years touring the world, telling of the blessing of a life of faith. Müller died at the age of ninety-three, leaving an estate valued at less than one thousand dollars. He had given back to the Institute almost one-half million dollars of personal gifts received during seventy years of ministry.

# Absalom Backus Earle

## (1812–1895)

A. B. Earle was born in Charlton, New York. He was converted at the age of sixteen and began preaching two years later. He spent the next three years studying and preaching. At the age of twenty-one he was ordained at Amsterdam, New York. After pastoring there for five years, Earle felt led by the Lord to enter the evangelistic ministry. The next fifty-eight years of his life were spent holding meetings in the United States (every state) and Canada. He held 39,330 services, traveled 370,000 miles, led 160,000 souls to Christ, and earned a total of $65,520 for his sixty-four years of ministry. He influenced 400 men to enter the ministry.

Earle authored the following books: *Bringing in the Sheaves, Abiding Peace, Rest of Faith, The Human Will, The Work of an Evangelist, Evidences of Conversion,* and *Winning Souls.* He died at his home in Newton, Massachusetts, March 30, 1895, at the age of eighty-three.

A writer in a leading British religious paper said concerning Mr. Earle: "His preaching was not eloquent. His delivery was not beyond the average. His voice had no special power. His large angular frame and passionless mouth were decidedly against him. His sermons seemed sometimes as though composed thirty years ago, before we so often heard, as now, the more clear and ringing utterances of free grace, and the name of Jesus in almost every sentence. He expressed his own emotions very simply, and did not often refer to them. His rhetoric was often at fault, and sometimes his grammar. Truly the enticing words of man's wisdom were wanting in his case.

"Coming to the meeting perfectly free to follow the guidance of the Spirit, the preacher seemed as simple and as easily guided in any direction as the smallest child in the house. The congregation, which seemed to be so wonderfully swayed by him, were really controlled by the same Holy Spirit which controlled him. He simply watched for and recognized the guidance of God, and walked in it. . . .

"There was no rule in his movements. He sometimes asked the awakened to come forward, sometimes to rise in their seats; sometimes no expression was called for. All was simple and natural; and the very simplicity itself, and the unexpectedness of the direction of the meetings, surprised the unconverted out of their defences."

Earle was a Baptist, but he was strongly in favor of union meetings in evangelistic work. He believed that one of the most potent factors in bringing souls to Christ was the sight of Christians of different denominations working together in perfect harmony.

Earle was a strong believer in the preaching of future punishment.

"I have found by long experience," says he, "that the severest threatenings of the law of God have a prominent place in leading men to Christ. They must see themselves LOST before they will cry for mercy. They will not escape from danger until they see it. I have reason to believe that a single sermon I have often preached on 'The Sin that Hath Never Forgiveness' (Mark 3:29), has been the means of more than twenty thousand conversions." He also says, concerning this sermon: "I have known scores to give themselves to Christ under a single sermon on this subject, again and again." "The wicked never flee from 'the wrath to come' until they are fully satisfied there is wrath," says he.

# David Livingstone

## (1813–1873)

David Livingstone was born the son of deeply religious but humble parents, who lived near Glasgow, Scotland. He studied medicine and theology at the University of Glasgow. Livingstone tried to go to China as a missionary in 1838, but when the Opium War in China closed the doors, he went to South Africa. He had been challenged by Robert Moffat, a missionary to that country, who said, "On a clear morning the smoke of a thousand villages could be seen where the name of Christ had never been heard." He joined Moffat and married his daughter. Livingstone pushed two hundred miles north of Moffat's assigned station and founded another mission station, Mabosta. Livingstone continued on the mission field and advanced fourteen hundred miles into the interior in spite of the hardships. His purpose was to open the door of Africa to the Gospel. He was attacked and maimed by a lion, his home was destroyed during the Boer War, his body was often racked by fever and dysentery, and his wife died on the field. One morning in May, 1873, a faithful native found Livingstone by his bed, kneeling and dead. The natives buried his heart in Africa as he had requested, but his body was returned to England and buried in Westminster Abbey.

Many felt no single African explorer had done so much for African geography as Livingstone during his thirty years' work. His travels covered one-third of the continent, from the Cape to near the Equator, and from the Atlantic to the Indian Ocean. Livingstone was no hurried traveler; he did his journeying leisurely, carefully observing and recording with the eye of a trained scientific observer. His example and his death acted like an inspiration, filling Africa with an army of explorers and missionaries, and raising in Europe so powerful a feeling against the slave trade that through him slavery may be considered as having received its death blow.

Henry M. Stanley, a newspaper correspondent sent by *The New York Herald*, set out to find Livingstone after he had not been heard from for a long period of time. Stanley was so impressed with Livingstone that after his death he carried on mission work, leading the king of Buganda to Christ.

# John Gibson Paton
## (1824–1907)

John G. Paton was born near Dumfries, Scotland. Later his family moved to Torthorwald, where, in a humble thatched cottage of three rooms, his parents reared five sons and six daughters. The middle room of the cottage was known as the "sanctuary," for it was there that John's father went three times a day to pour out his heart in prayer to God for the needs of the family. At the age of twelve, John was helping his father in the stocking business but also studying Latin and Greek. Later he left home to study medicine and theology in Glasgow. Not long after, he became a missionary to the poor in the slums of Glasgow. The work was discouraging, but during ten years of faithful labor, Paton won many to Christ, including eight boys who later became ministers. When John was about thirty years old, the Reformed Church of Scotland asked for a missionary to help with the work in the New Hebrides Islands. John answered the call, and soon he and his new bride were on their way to the South Pacific in spite of the news that the previous missionaries had been murdered and eaten by cannibals. The Patons settled on the island of Tanna and began their ministry. Since the natives had no written language, John communicated with them in sign language. Gradually he learned a few native words and after many months mastered their language and reduced it to writing. While there, his wife and infant son contacted a tropical fever and died. The natives repeatedly stole his equipment, his life was in constant danger, but still Paton remained and preached to them. Moving to the island of Aniwa, Paton built a home, a mission headquarters, two orphanages, a church, and a schoolhouse, and after many years of patient ministry, the entire island professed Christianity. In 1899 he saw his Aniwa New Testament printed and missionaries on twenty-five of the thirty islands of the New Hebrides. He went to be with the Lord in 1907.

HENLEY

# William Bramwell Booth

## (1829–1912)

William Booth was born in Nottingham, England. He was converted to Christ through the efforts of a Methodist minister and soon
became interested in working with the outcasts and poor people of
Nottingham. Booth preached on the streets and made hundreds of
hospital calls before he was twenty years of age. From 1850 to 1861
he served as a pastor in the Methodist church, after which he and his
wife left the church and stepped out by faith in evangelistic work in
East London. There he organized the East London Christian Revival Society. Out of this beginning came the Salvation Army, with
its uniforms, organization and discipline. By 1930 there were branches
of the Army in fifty-five countries. Its main emphasis under General
Booth was street preaching, personal evangelism and practical philanthropy. More than two million derelicts have professed faith in the
Lord Jesus Christ through the work of the Salvation Army since its
founding by the General.

## From *In Darkest England, the Way Out*

*To get a man soundly saved it is not enough to put on him a pair
of new breeches, to give him regular work, or even to give him a
university education. . . .*

*To change the nature of the individual, to get at the heart, to save
his soul is the only real, lasting method of doing him any good. In
many modern schemes of social regeneration it is forgotten that "it
takes a soul to move a body, e'en to a cleaner sty," and at the risk
of being misunderstood and misrepresented, I must assert in the most
unqualified way that it is primarily and mainly for the sake of saving
the soul that I seek the salvation of the body.*

*But what is the use of preaching the Gospel to men whose whole at-
tention is concentrated upon a mad, desperate struggle to keep themselves alive? You might as well give a tract to a shipwrecked sailor
who is battling with the surf which has drowned his comrades and
threatens to drown him. He will not listen to you. Nay, he cannot
hear you any more than a man whose head is under water can listen to a sermon. The first thing to do is to get him at least a foot-
ing on firm ground, and to give him room to live. Then you may
have a chance. At present you have none. And you will have all
the better opportunity to find a way to his heart, if he comes to know
that it was you who pulled him out of the horrible pit and the miry
clay in which he was sinking to perdition.*

116

# Thomas DeWitt Talmage

## (1832–1902)

An extremely prolific writer and preacher, Talmage has been one of the most popular and most widely read of the preachers from the late nineteenth and early twentieth centuries.

Talmage was a "country boy" of humble, pious parentage. Born at Bound Brook, New Jersey, he was the last of twelve children. Even as a youth he possessed such gifts as a fervent imagination, fondness of nature's charms, unusual powers of expression, a manner dramatic in the highest degree, a mature vivaciousness, electric and spontaneous. Already at this age others had begun to predict great things for him. He graduated from the University of New York with distinction. He began a course of study for the legal profession but after a year he felt the need to pursue the work of the Lord and entered the New Brunswick Theological Seminary connected with Rutgers College. He was converted at age eighteen and united with the Dutch Reformed Church. Talmage says of his youth:

> I had many sound thrashings when I was a boy (not as many as I ought to have had, for I was the last child, and my parents let me off), but the most memorable scene in my childhood was that of father and mother at morning and evening prayers. I cannot forget it, for I used often to be squirming around on the floor and looking at them while they were praying.

During the Civil War he served as chaplain in the Union Army. In 1869 he became pastor of the Central Presbyterian Church of Brooklyn, New York. This decision was a difficult one since the request came at the same time as four others, all of which were larger churches. Brooklyn, a failing church of only nineteen remaining members, grew so under his ministry that within a year a new building, known as the Brooklyn Tabernacle, was erected. That building was destroyed by fire in 1872, but it was rebuilt. It also burned to the ground, as did a third church building.

Talmage was known as a lecturer as well as a clergyman. He had a fine, erect figure, strong, clear-cut features, and a winning manner,

## Thomas DeWitt Talmage

and he always used many startling gestures and illustrations to rivet attention. His critics called him a pulpit clown, but there were thousands who admired and reverenced him. He was editor of *The Christian at Work*, New York, (1873-1876), of *The Advance*, Chicago, (1877-1878), of *Frank Leslie's Sunday Magazine* (1879-1889), and of the *Christian Herald*, New York, from 1890.

The sermons of Talmage were printed in 3,500 newspapers each Sunday across America and Europe, and he authored a complete set of more than five hundred sermons. Preaching without the aid of notes, his oratorical powers were compared to those of George Whitefield and his poetic expression to that of Shakespeare and Milton.

### From the Sermon, "The A and the Z"

*Here is a long lane, overshadowed by fine trees, leading up to a mansion. What is the use of the lane if there were no mansion at the end? There is no use in the Old Testament except as a grand avenue to lead us up to the Gospel Dispensation. You may go early to a concert. Before the curtain is hoisted, you hear the musicians tuning up the violins, and getting ready all the instruments. After a while the curtain is hoisted, and the concert begins. All the statements, parables, orations, and miracles of the Old Testament were merely preparatory, and when all was ready, in the time of Christ, the curtain hoists, and there pours forth the Oratorio of the Messiah — all nations joining in the Hallelujah Chorus.*

*Moses, in his account of the creation, shows the platform on which Christ was to act. Prophets and apostles took subordinate parts in the tragedy. The first act was a manger and a Babe; the last a cross and its Victim. The Bethlehem star in the first scenery shifted for the crimson upholstery of a crucifixion. Earth, and Heaven, and Hell the spectators. Angels applauding in the galleries; devils hissing in the pit.*

*Christ is the Beginning and the End of the Bible.*

*In Genesis, who was Isaac, bound amid the fagots? Type of*

Christ, the ALPHA. In Revelation, what was the Water of life? Christ, the OMEGA. In Genesis, what was the ladder over Jacob's pillow? Christ, the ALPHA. In Revelation, who was the Conqueror on the white horse? Christ, the OMEGA. In Exodus, what was the Smitten Rock? Christ, the ALPHA. In Revelation, who was the Lamb before the throne? Christ, the OMEGA. Take Christ out of this book, and there are other books I would rather have than the Bible. Take Him out, and you have the Louvre without the pictures; you have the Tower of London without the jewels. Take Him out, and man is a failure, and the world a carcass, and eternity a vast horror.

When the world broke loose, the only hand swung out to catch it was that of Jesus. At Long Branch, on the beach, on a summer's day, hundreds of people are sporting; but suddenly someone cries, "Look there! A man is drowning." Out of hundreds, perhaps there is only one strong swimmer. He plunges in, and brings the man safely ashore. On the beach of Heaven, one day, there sat myriads of immortals, merry with a great gladness; but the voice of one of the immortals cried out, "See there! A world is drowning! To the rescue! Where are the wreckers? Launch the lifeboats! Who will go?"

Angels did not dare venture. Heaven itself stands helpless before the scene. It knows how to wave a palm or shout in a coronation, but not how to take out of the floods a drowning world. Jesus bounds from the throne, and throws His robe on one side, His crown on the other. Swift as a roe on the mountains, He comes down over the hills. The shining ones stand back as He says, "Lo! I come." Amid the wrathful surges He beats His way out to the dying world; and while, out in the deep waters, with bloody agony He wrestled with it, and it seemed for a little while uncertain whether it would take Him down or He would lift it up, those on the beach trembled, and in an hour grew ages older; and when at last, in His great strength, He lifted it in His right hand and brought it back, there went up a hosanna from all the cloud of witnesses. He began the work, and He shall complete it. Ring all the bells of earth and Heaven today in honor of Christ the ALPHA and Christ the OMEGA!

121

# James Hudson Taylor

## (1832–1905)

James Hudson Taylor was born on May 21, 1832, at Barnsley, England, the son of a Methodist minister. Through Christian training received from his parents, Taylor was endowed with strength of character, resoluteness, unshakeable faith in God, determination for duty, love, and consideration for others. Because he was a weak and frail boy, he received his early training from his parents. His father had desired to become a missionary to China and prayed that his son might go in his place. Even at the age of four, James was heard to say, "When I am a man I will be a missionary and go to China." He experienced conversion at the age of seventeen.

After studying medicine and theology, Taylor went to China in 1854 as a missionary under the auspices of the China Evangelization Society. In 1858 after working in a hospital for four years, he married the daughter of another missionary. He returned to England in 1860 and spent five years translating the New Testament into the Ningpo dialect. He was extremely able in sharing his vision of the missionary enterprise, and God used him to establish the China Inland Mission in 1866. This was strictly a *faith* mission and became the subsequent pattern for many of the faith missions of today. In 1870 his wife and two of their children died of cholera. He later remarried to Miss Faulding. The rest of his life was spent in recruiting missionaries around the world but particularly in England and North America. He was in and out of China on numerous occasions. Before his death he established 205 mission stations with 849 missionaries from England and 125,000 witnessing Chinese Christians. His ability to motivate people to give themselves and their possessions to the cause of Christ was significant. He died in Changsha, China, in 1905.

Hudson Taylor expressed his personal commitment to God,

*Let me tell you how God answered the prayers of my dear mother, and of my beloved sister, now Mrs. Broomhall, for my conversion. On a day which I shall never forget, when I was about seventeen years of age, my dear mother being absent from home, I had a holiday, and in the afternoon looked through my father's library to find some book with which to while away the unoccupied hours. Nothing attracting me, I turned over a little basket of pamphlets, and selected from amongst them a Gospel tract which looked interesting, saying to myself, "There will be a story at the commencement, and a sermon or moral at the close: I will take the former and leave the latter for those who like it."*

*I sat down to read the little book in an utterly unconcerned state of mind, believing indeed at the time that if there were any salvation it was not for me, and with a distinct intention to put away the tract as soon as it should seem prosy. I may say that it was not uncommon in those days to call conversion "becoming serious," and judging by the faces of some of its professors, it appeared to be a very serious matter indeed.*

*. . . Little did I know at the time what was going on in the heart of my dear mother, seventy or eighty miles away. She rose from the dinner table that afternoon with an intense yearning for the conversion of her boy, and feeling that — absent from home, and having more leisure than she could otherwise secure — a special opportunity was afforded her of pleading with God on my behalf. She went to her room and turned the key in the door, resolved not to leave that spot until her prayers were answered. Hour after hour did that dear mother plead for me, until at length she could pray no longer, but was constrained to praise God for that which His Spirit taught her had already been accomplished — the conversion of her only son.*

*I, in the meantime, had been led in the way I have mentioned to take up this little tract, and while reading it was struck with the sentence, "The finished work of Christ." The thought passed through my mind, "Why does the author use this expression? Why not say the atoning or propitiatory work of Christ?" Immediately the words*

## James Hudson Taylor

"It is finished" suggested themselves to my mind. What was finished? And I at once replied, "A full and perfect atonement and satisfaction for sin: the debt was paid by the Substitute; Christ died for our sins, and not for ours only, but also for the sins of the whole world." Then came the thought, "If the whole work was finished and the whole debt paid, what is there left for me to do?" And with this dawned the joyful conviction, as light was flashed into my soul by the Holy Spirit, that there was nothing in the world to be done but to fall on one's knees, and accepting this Saviour and His salvation, to praise Him for evermore. Thus while my dear mother was praising God on her knees in her chamber, I was praising Him in the old warehouse to which I had gone alone to read at my leisure this little book.

Several days elapsed ere I ventured to make my beloved sister the confidante of my joy, and then only after she had promised not to tell anyone of my soul secret. When our dear mother came home a fortnight later, I was the first to meet her at the door, and to tell her I had such glad news to give. I can almost feel that dear mother's arms around my neck, as she pressed me to her bosom and said, "I know, my boy; I have been rejoicing for a fortnight in the glad tidings you have to tell me." "Why," I asked in surprise, "has Amelia broken her promise? She said she would tell no one." My dear mother assured me that it was not from any human source that she had learned the tidings and went on to tell the little incident mentioned above. You will agree with me that it would be strange indeed if I were not a believer in the power of prayer.

Nor was this all. Some little time after, I picked up a pocket-book exactly like one of my own, and thinking that it was mine, opened it. The lines that caught my eye were an entry in the little diary, which belonged to my sister, to the effect that she would give herself daily to prayer until God should answer in the conversion of her brother. Exactly one month later the Lord was pleased to turn me from darkness to light.

124

# Charles Haddon Spurgeon

## (1834–1892)

Many have declared Spurgeon to be the greatest preacher since the apostle Paul. He was an English Baptist preacher born at Kelvedon, Essex, June 19, 1834. His father was an independent minister. After attending Colchester school, young Charles was appointed usher in a school at Newmarket in 1849 and formally joined the Baptists in 1850. He was converted at age sixteen, and immediately began preaching. Spurgeon's extraordinary ability was immediately recognized and he began pastoring the first church in 1852. In 1854 he took a small deteriorating church in South London. At once throngs of people were attracted to the small church. After moving several times (1859–1861) the congregation finally built the great Metropolitan Tabernacle, seating six thousand people. Here Spurgeon, who had become the most popular preacher in London, had his pulpit for the rest of his life.

Spurgeon was a convinced Calvinist. He repudiated baptismal regeneration, and distrusted the rising tendencies of modern Biblical criticism. Beginning in 1855, he published a sermon each week. In 1865 he began to edit the monthly *Sword and Trowel*. He excelled not only in preaching but also in public prayer. His membership included over five thousand, and it is said that he knew them all by name. He observed the Lord's Supper almost every Sunday either at home or in the tabernacle. He led in the establishment of many benevolent institutions.

Spurgeon always appealed to the Scriptures as authoritative, and his sermons were based on Old Testament texts as well as those from the New Testament. His simplicity and his voice were great assets to preaching. Spurgeon excelled in his use of illustrations and anecdotes. He was criticized in his own day for his use of illustration, but like Jesus, Spurgeon believed in appealing to both eye and ear. He looked on the Gospel as a "gift of God to the imagination." In one particular lecture he said that a sermon without illustration is like a house without windows.

Wilbur Chapman came to see the secret of Spurgeon's power. Spurgeon said to him,

> Everyday and night thousands of men and women here in London pray for the work of the Tabernacle, and for me. All around the world, day after day, hundreds of thousands of God's people ask for His blessing on me and my sermons. In answer to those prayers the Lord opens the windows of heaven and pours out so many blessings that there is not room in our hearts and lives to receive them all. Young man, try this way of running your church!

Before his death in 1892 he had published more than two thousand sermons and forty-nine volumes of commentaries, sayings, anecdotes, illustrations, and devotions.

## From the Sermon, "Songs in the Night"

. . . *One word of God is like a piece of gold, and the Christian is the gold-beater, and he can hammer that promise out for whole weeks. I can say myself, I have lived on one promise for weeks, and want no other. I want just simply to hammer that promise out into goldleaf, and plate my whole existence with joy from it. The Christian gets his songs from God: God gives him inspiration, and teaches him how to sing: "God my Maker, who giveth songs in the night."*

*So, then, poor Christian, thou needst not go pumping up thy poor heart to make it glad. Go to thy Maker, and ask him to give thee a song in the night. Thou art a poor dry well: thou hast heard it said, that when a pump is dry, you must pour water down it first of all, and then you will get some up; and so, Christian, when thou art dry, go to God, ask him to pour some joy down thee, and then thou wilt get some joy up from thine own heart. Do not go to this comforter or that, for you will find them Job's comforters, after all; but go*

## Charles Haddon Spurgeon

thou first and foremost to thy Maker, for he is the great composer of songs and teacher of music; he it is who can teach thee how to sing: "God, my Maker, who giveth me songs in the night."

. . . Go back, man; sing of that moment, and then thou wilt have a song in the night. Or if thou hast almost forgotten that, then sure thou hast some precious milestone along the road of life that is not quite grown over with moss, on which thou canst read some happy inscription of his mercy toward thee! What! didst thou never have a sickness like that which thou art suffering now, and did he not raise thee up from that? Wast thou never poor before, and did he not supply thy wants? Wast thou never in straits before, and did he not deliver thee? Come, man! I beseech thee, go to the river of thine experience, and pull up a few bulrushes, and weave them into an ark, wherein thine infant faith may float safely on the stream. I bid thee not forget what God hath done. What! hast thou buried thine own diary? I beseech thee, man, turn over the book of thy remembrance. Canst thou not see some sweet hill Mizar? Canst thou not think of some blessed hour when the Lord met with thee at Hermon? Hast thou never been on the Delectable Mountains? Hast thou never escaped the jaw of the lion and the paw of the bear? Nay, O man, I know thou hast; go back, then, a little way, and take the mercies of yesterday, and they shall glitter through the darkness, and thou shalt find that God hath given thee a song in the night. . . .

Thy head may be crowned with thorny troubles now, but it shall wear a starry crown directly; thy hand may be filled with cares — it shall grasp a harp soon, a harp full of music. Thy garments may be soiled with dust now; they shall be white by-and-by. Wait a little longer. Ah! beloved, how despicable our troubles and trials will seem when we look back upon them! Looking at them here in the prospect, they seem immense; but when we get to heaven, we shall then,

With transporting joys, recount
The labors of our feet.

# Adoniram Judson Gordon

## (1836–1895)

Adoniram Judson Gordon was born in New Hampton, New Hampshire, on April 13, 1836. His parents were Christians. His youth was characterized by hard work in his father's woolen mill, long walks to school, and a devout church life. At about age fifteen Adoniram was converted to Christ. Soon after his conversion he was baptized and received into the church. A year later he felt the call of God to the ministry.

He attended nearby New London Academy and then Brown University. In 1860 he entered the Newton Theological Seminary. Upon graduation in 1863 he accepted the call to be a Baptist pastor at Jamaica Plain, near Boston. For six years he pastored this church while he grew in his spiritual experience. In 1869 he accepted the call to the Clarendon Street Baptist Church in Boston. He remained there for more than a quarter of a century.

In 1878 he began editing the *Watchword,* a monthly magazine, and in 1888 he became chairman of the Executive Committee of the American Baptist Missionary Union (since 1910, the American Baptist Foreign Missionary Society). In 1889 he founded the Boston Missionary Training School (now Gordon College and Divinity School).

Gordon saw the Clarendon Street Baptist Church completely transformed into one of the most spiritual and aggressive churches in America. He was also one of the most prominent leaders and speakers in Dwight Moody's great Northfield Conventions, and one year Moody left the convention entirely in his charge. In his *Ministry of the Spirit*, which is perhaps his greatest work, Dr. Gordon presents the work of the Holy Spirit in a three-fold aspect — sealing, filling, and anointing. Among his better known hymns are: "My Jesus, I Love Thee" and "I Shall See the King in His Beauty." On the morning of February 2, 1895, Dr. Gordon, with *Victory* as the last clearly audible word on his lips, fell asleep in Jesus.

## From the Book, *The Ministry of the Spirit*

*. . . that the presence of the personal Holy Spirit in the church was intended to be perpetual there can be no question. And whatsoever relations believers held to that Spirit in the beginning they have a right to claim to-day. We must withhold our consent from the inconsistent exegesis which would make the water baptism of the apostolic times still rigidly binding, but would relegate the baptism in the Spirit to a bygone dispensation. We hold indeed, that Pentecost was once for all, but equally that the appropriation of the Spirit by*

believers is always for all, and that the shutting up of certain great blessings of the Holy Ghost within that ideal realm called "the apostolic age," however convenient it may be as an escape from fancied difficulties, may be the means of robbing believers of some of their most precious covenant rights.

# Dwight Lyman Moody

## (1837–1899)

Undoubtedly one of the best-known and loved American evangelists, Dwight L. Moody was born in Northfield, Massachusetts, on
February 5, 1837. His father died when Dwight was four. Dwight's
formal education ended at age thirteen, and at seventeen he became
a clerk in his uncle's shoe store in Boston. Edward Kimble, his Sunday school teacher, led Moody to Christ in the shoe store. Moody
went to Chicago in 1856 and became a traveling salesman for a
wholesale shoe firm. He did extensive Sunday school recruitment in
his spare time and became affiliated with the YMCA in its early
years in Chicago. He resigned from business in 1860 to devote his
full time to the work of Christ. He married Emma Revell in 1862.

During the Civil War, Moody served with the United States Christian Commission, ministering to the troops on both sides, and often
was found at the front of battle. Here the eternal value of individuals
became clear to him and provided him with the impetus which later
enabled him to preach to adults. Moody became the president of
the YMCA of Chicago in 1866.

Moody organized and built an independent church in Chicago by
popular demand of those he led to Christ. In 1873 he went to England with Ira D. Sankey and held a series of revival meetings which
captured Britain. He left America virtually unknown in any national
sense and returned as a famed evangelist. Upon returning in August
of 1875 he made his home at Northfield, Massachusetts, his beloved
birthplace. During the next six years he conducted revivals all

across the United States. In 1879 he established the Northfield Seminary for Young Women and in 1881 the Mount Hermon School for Young Men.

In 1879 he was invited to return to England to conduct a second series of meetings. In 1884 he returned to do evangelistic work in America and Canada. In 1889 he founded the Chicago Bible Institute (now Moody Bible Institute), which has been a fountainhead for Christian workers throughout the world.

Moody was effective because of his love for the souls of men and his personal concern for their physical welfare. His preaching was known for its use of anecdotes and stories. Though not an educated man, Moody was respected by the educated. It is claimed that over one million people were converted to Jesus Christ during his ministry. His work continues today through the Moody Memorial Church and the Moody Bible Institute of Chicago.

## From the Sermon, "Heaven"

*We have for our subject this evening, heaven. It is not as some talk about heaven, as just the air. I find a good many people now that think there is no heaven, only just here in this world; that this is all the heaven we will ever see. I talked with a man the other day, who said he thought there is nothing to justify us in believing there is any other heaven than that which we are in now. Well, if*

# Dwight Lyman Moody

this is heaven, it is a very strange kind of heaven — this world of sickness, and sorrow, and sin. If he thinks this is really all the heaven we are going to see, he has a queer idea of it. There are three heavens spoken of in the Bible, and the Hebrews acknowledge in their writings three heavens. The first is the aerial — the air, the wind, the air that the birds fly in; that is one heaven. Then, there is the heaven of the firmament, where the stars are; and then there is the heaven of heavens, where God's throne is and the mansions of the Lord are — the mansions of light and peace, the home of the blessed, the home of the Redeemer, where the angels dwell. That is the heaven that we believe in, and the heaven that we want to talk about today.

The sanctified man and the unsanctified one look at heaven very differently. The unsanctified man simply chooses heaven in preference to hell. He thinks that if he must go to either one he would rather try heaven. It is like a man with a farm who has a place offered him in another country, where there is said to be a gold mine; he hates to give up all he has and take any risk. But if he is going to be banished, and must leave, and has his choice of living in a wilderness or digging in a coal pit, or else take the gold mine, then there is no hesitation. The unregenerate man likes heaven better than hell, but he likes this world best of all. The true believer prizes heaven above everything else, and is always willing to give up the world. Everybody wants to enjoy heaven after they die, but they don't want to be heavenly-minded while they live.

134

RUCKMAN

# Jeremiah McAuley

## (1839–1884)

Jerry McAuley was born in 1839 in County Kerry, Ireland. His father was a counterfeiter who fled home to escape the law. At the age of thirteen, Jerry was sent to America to live with a married sister in New York City. Soon he was a member of a gang on Water Street and supporting himself by stealing. His life of crime seemed to intensify with each offense. Finally, he was arrested and sentenced to fifteen years in Sing Sing Prison. While in prison, McAuley began to read the Bible in search of forgiveness for his sins. After reading the Bible through twice, he accepted Christ through the efforts of a lady missionary who visited the prison. His prayer of repentance was sincere because of the guilt associated with his former life. His attitude and conduct changed so much that he was released from prison in 1864 after serving seven years and two months. In October, 1872, McAuley, his wife, and a few helpers opened the Water Street Mission in the heart of the slum section of New York City. Night after night many of the seats were filled with drunks and transients looking for a place to rest and relief from the cold. His former life of crime on Water Street and his conversion were his credentials for preaching. He enjoyed great success in those he reached with the Gospel. McAuley's mission accepted anyone, regardless of how dirty he looked, how foul he smelled, or how uncertainly he stood to his feet. The services of the mission were not limited to the physical needs of the men, as Gospel meetings were conducted nightly. Singing, testimonies, and preaching competed with the shouts and noises of the Water Street slums. The Water Street Mission, under McAuley's direction, became an example of Christian compassion for the down and out. Tens of thousands of transients, drunks, and harlots heard the Gospel of Jesus Christ, many of them responding to the invitation. The popular knowledge of McAuley's work was so widespread that a year after his death his work was mentioned in secular sociology books as representative of mission work. McAuley was respected by the "transient" on skid row, as well as ministers and businessmen. Although McAuley died in 1884, his influence lived on through the work of the mission.

# Benajah Harvey Carroll

## (1843–1914)

B. H. Carroll was born in Carrollton, Mississippi, the son of a preacher-farmer and one of twelve children. At the age of eighteen he graduated from Waco University, Texas, and spent the next four years in the Confederate Army during the Civil War. In 1865, at the age of twenty-two, he was converted to Christ in a woodshed through the efforts of a Methodist evangelist. He was ordained to the Gospel ministry one year later. During the first years of his ministry, immigrants were moving into Texas by the thousands, and Carroll labored for their evangelization. After pastoring several Baptist churches, he became Secretary of the Education Commission of the Baptist General Convention of Texas in 1899. He acted in this capacity until 1901, when he became head of the Bible department at Baylor Theological Seminary, which later became Southwestern Baptist Theological Seminary. Dr. Carroll served as president of Southwestern from 1908 until his death in 1914. In addition to his intellectual and argumentative abilities in an age of denominational debates, he possessed a lovable nature. He once said, "When I come to know a man and love him as a friend and a brother, nothing can destroy the tie that binds our hearts in Christian love." He believed in the Baptist interpretation of the teachings of the New Testament and was devoted to spreading those teachings to the uttermost parts of the earth.

## From *The Four Gospels*

*The prayers of God's people, so it seems to me from the teachings of the Bible, are the appointed means, the means which he has designated — clearly and unmistakably designated — for bringing about revivals of religion. And yet even here we confront an insuperable difficulty if we leave out God's absolute sovereignty. The difficulty can be best stated by an illustration: Water from above must be poured down a pump long dry before it can pump up water from below. We work the pump handle in vain. We go through the motion, but it will not draw. So a drought comes into the soul. Our graces languish. We try to pray and are conscious of failure. In one scripture it is stated as a reason why such weak instrumentalities are employed that no flesh shall glory in God's presence, that it should become manifest to angels in heaven and devils in hell and men on earth that power belongeth to God; that the Lord, he is mighty and no other is great. It is with God, and with God alone.*

# Albert Benjamin Simpson

## (1884–1919)

The fourth of nine children, Albert Simpson was born December 15, 1844, at Cavendish, Prince Edward Island, Canada. His parents were Scottish. Concerning his early religious experience he says, "My first definite religious crisis came about fourteen years of age. Prior to this I had for a good while been planning to study for the ministry. There grew up in my young heart a great conflict about my future life; naturally I rebelled against the ministry because of the restraints which it would put upon many pleasures. One irresistible desire was to have a gun and to shoot and hunt; and I reasoned that if I were a minister, it would never do for me to indulge in such pastimes." The young Simpson saved his money and purchased a shot gun and hid it from the family, sneaking off now and then to hunt. When discovered he says, "It was a day of judgment; and when that wicked weapon was brought from its hiding place, I stood crushed and confounded as I was sentenced to the deep humiliation of returning it to the man from whom I bought it, losing not only my gun but my money.

"That tragedy settled the question of the ministry. I soon decided to give up all side issues and prepare myself if I could only find a way to preach the Gospel."

His father talked to his eldest son and Albert, telling them he only had enough money to send one through school to prepare for the ministry. It was the duty of Albert to stay home so his older brother could attend. Crushed, Albert agreed but asked if he could attend if he found his own means of support. He received his father's blessing.

Albert became quite ill, and during this trying period his conversion to Christ took place.

140

In 1861 Simpson entered Knox College located on the campus of the University of Toronto. He managed to earn his way through college by teaching and preaching and also won several awards and scholarships in competition. He was ordained September 12, 1865, after successfully completing college, and accepted his first pastorate in Knox Church, Hamilton, Ontario, Canada. Simpson was married the following day.

Later Simpson accepted the call to serve as pastor of the Chestnut Street Presbyterian Church in Louisville, Kentucky. His work there prospered, and a tabernacle was erected for the purpose of evangelistic services which grew out of Sunday evening services held outside his own church. One incident reflects his pastoral work: Simpson felt compelled to visit a man late one evening during a storm, and the gentleman was so impressed with Simpson's concern that he was converted to Christ that night.

In 1881 Simpson founded an independent Gospel tabernacle in New York. There he published the *Alliance Weekly* and wrote seventy books on Christian living. A number of mission works were started by workers influenced by his ministry.

A major portion of Dr. Simpson's ministry involved conventions. They had the fervor of camp meetings, evangelistic campaigns, and missionary convocations. Out of these missionary societies, first the Evangelical Missionary Alliance, and eventually the Christian and Missionary Alliance came into being.

Dr. Simpson was a man of action, a leader, an author and editor, and a man of prayer. Regarding prayer he said, "An important help in the life of prayer is the habit of bringing everything to God, mo-

141

## Albert Benjamin Simpson

ment by moment, as it comes to us in life." Albert Benjamin Simpson died October 29, 1919.

### From *The Life of A. B. Simpson*

. . . *My life seemed to hang upon a thread, for I had the hope that God would spare me long enough to find salvation if I only continued to seek it with all my heart. At length one day, in the library of my old minister and teacher, I stumbled upon an old musty volume called* Marshall's Gospel Mystery of Sanctification. *As I turned the leaves, my eyes fell upon a sentence which opened for me the gates of life eternal. "The first good work you will ever perform is to believe on the Lord Jesus Christ. Until you do this, all your works, prayers, tears, and good resolutions are vain. To believe on the Lord Jesus is just to believe that He saves you here and now, for He has said — 'Him that cometh to me I will in no wise cast out.' The moment you do this, you will pass into eternal life, you will be justified from all your sins, and receive a new heart and all the gracious operations of the Holy Spirit."*

*To my poor bewildered soul this was like the light from heaven that fell upon Saul of Tarsus on his way to Damascus. I immediately fell upon my knees, and looking up to the Lord, I said, "Lord Jesus, Thou hast said — Him that cometh to me I will in no wise cast out. Thou knowest how long and earnestly I have tried to come, but I did not know how. Now I come the best I can, and I dare to believe that Thou dost receive me and save me, and that I am now Thy child, forgiven and saved simply because I have taken Thee at Thy word. Abba Father, Thou art mine, and I am Thine."*

142

# Cyrus Ingersoll Scofield

## (1843–1921)

Born in Lenawee County, Michigan, August 19, 1843, Cyrus Scofield became one of the foremost names among Bible students. His mother died at his birth, but before she died she prayed that this boy might become a minister. This was not told to Cyrus until after he entered the ministry. His family moved to Tennessee, where he received his early education.

As a boy, Cyrus had a thirst for knowledge and was exceedingly thorough in his investigations. Whenever he came upon a person or event of which he knew little, he would pursue the subject until he became knowledgeable concerning it. This prepared him to become a competent scholar later in life. Although his parents were Christian and the Bible was read in the home, Cyrus didn't consider it a book for investigative study but one to enjoy merely for its stories. His religious experience prior to conversion was superficial.

The Civil War prevented him from entering the university and he never did receive a formal collegiate education. At seventeen he entered the Confederate Army, and because he was an excellent horseman he became an orderly. He frequently carried messages under gunfire. The Confederate Cross of Honor was awarded him for bravery at Antietam.

When the war was over, Scofield studied law in St. Louis, and afterward moved to Kansas, where he was admitted to the bar in 1869. He served in the Kansas State Legislature and at the age of twenty-nine was appointed by President Grant as United States District Attorney for Kansas. Later he returned to St. Louis and re-entered law practice. During this time he began to drink heavily. However, this passion for drink was completely removed when he received Jesus Christ through the efforts of Thomas S. McPheeters, a YMCA worker.

Scofield immediately became active in Christian work. He was ordained in Dallas, Texas, October 1883, where he began his ministry as pastor of the First Congregational Church.

As a result of diligent and systematic study of the Scriptures during his years of ministry, he produced the Scofield Reference Bible and the Scofield Bible Correspondence Course.

Through the influence of private talks with Hudson Taylor of the China-Inland Mission and also a book by a brilliant journalist-traveler, William Eleroy Curtis, Scofield felt God directing his attention toward the Central American region for missionary activity. The church at Dallas began giving more to missionary work than to the home work. They established the Central American Mission in 1890.

Concerning the Reference Bible, he asked himself this question: "What kind of reference Bible would have helped me most when I was first trying to learn something of the Word of God, but ignorant of the very first principles of Bible study?" This was a tremendous undertaking and took a great deal of tedious work and genius. He and his wife made trips to England and the continent while completing the work. The Oxford libraries were opened to him, and the Oxford University Press published it. It was completed in 1907 and presented to the public in January 1909.

In reflecting upon his own lifetime Scofield recalls the two great epochs of his life: "The first was when I ceased to take as final human teachings about the Bible and went to the Bible itself. The second was when I found Christ as Victory and Achievement."

Scofield died on Sunday morning July 24, 1921, at Douglaston, Long Island. Hundreds of thousands now appreciate and use his famous Scofield Reference Bible.

## From a Letter to Charles Trumbull, Scofield's Biographer

. . . *Such successes as I achieved in my life in the world of selfish*

## Cyrus Ingersoll Scofield

*aspiration might easily be made so prominent in my life story as to leave my conversion an event like the others. I owe it to the Lord and to my boundless indebtedness to His grace to do what I may to correct the notion that it was a brilliantly successful man who, in my person, came to Christ.*

*Great opportunities had indeed been given me, and for years I made them my own. But slowly, insidiously, the all but universal habit of drink in the society and among the men of my time overmastered me. It was not a victor in the battle of life — though victories had come to him — but a ruined and hopeless man who, despite all his struggles, was fast bound in chains of his own forging. He had no thought of Christ other than a vague respect, the survival of a family influence. There was no hope that in a church some time he might hear and believe the Gospel, for he never went to church.*

*And then Jesus Christ took up the case. Men were beginning to turn away from him, but the Lord of glory sought him. Through Thomas McPheeters, a joyous, hopeful soul, Jesus Christ offered Himself to that wreck.*

*It was a Bible conversion. From a worn pocket Testament McPheeters read to me the great Gospel passages, the great deliverance passages, John 3:16; 6:47; 10:28; Acts 13:38, 39, and the like. And when I asked, like the Philippian jailer of old, "What must I do to be saved?" he just read them again, and we knelt, and I received Jesus Christ as my Saviour. And — oh! Trumbull, put it into the story, put it big and plain: instantly the chains were broken never to be forged again — the passion for drink was taken away. Put it "Instantly," dear Trumbull. Make it plain. Don't say: "He strove with his drink-sin and came off victor." He did nothing of the kind. Divine power did it, wholly of grace. To Christ be all the glory.*

146

# Samuel Porter Jones

## (1847–1906)

Sam Jones was born at Oak Bowrey, Alabama, in 1847 and was reared at Cartersville, Georgia. He studied to be a lawyer, but drinking and gambling brought him to the brink of ruin. At his father's deathbed, he fell on his knees, repented of his sin, and trusted Christ as his personal Saviour. He preached his first sermon one week later and was licensed to preach in the Methodist church only three months after his conversion. He served several pastorates, but gained fame as a lecturer and evangelist, conducting campaigns in some of America's largest cities.

His success seems to have rested almost entirely on his mastery of audiences — a mastery so long and often proved as to compel his recognition as perhaps the foremost American public speaker of his generation. The secret of his mastery seems to have been in part his physical and moral courage and in part his understanding of the common man's dislike of sham and hypocrisy and delight in hearing them exposed and condemned in homely words and epigrammatic style.

A year before his death Sam Jones was called to the speaker's platform in Atlanta by President Theodore Roosevelt, who said to him, "Sam, you have been doing as a private citizen what I have tried to do as a public servant." The vast audience cheered. His funeral in Georgia in 1906 was an affair of state. Much of the wit of Will Rogers is traceable to Sam Jones. Well over five-hundred thousand people were converted to Christ as a result of his ministry.

## From the Sermon, "Eternal Damnation"

*And yonder is the old ship Humanity, and now the waves of God's wrath and judgment begin to pitch and toss her and drive her on the rocks, and she is about to go down forever, when the Son of God sees her; and I see him come from the shining shores of heaven, as swift as the morning light, and throw His arms around this old, sinking ship. She carries him under three days and nights, and He brings her to the surface on the third morning; and then God grasps the stylus and signs the Magna Charta of man's salvation, and then at the blessed moment it is written: "'Whosoever believeth in the Son of God shall not perish, but have everlasting life."*

# Reuben Archer Torrey

## (1856–1928)

Torrey was born on January 28, 1856, in Hoboken, New Jersey. He was an educated man, having graduated from both Yale University and Seminary. In addition he studied at Leipzig and Erlangen Universities in Germany. Torrey was ordained a Congregational minister in 1878 and was superintendent of the Minneapolis City Mission Society. In 1889 he was called to Chicago to supervise the Moody Bible Institute and be pastor of the Moody Memorial Church until 1908.

Most widely known as an evangelist, Torrey made a world-wide tour of evangelism, resulting in one hundred thousand professions of faith in the Lord Jesus Christ.

Torrey was an excellent educator and much of the credit for the success of Moody Bible Institute is attributed to his able leadership. He was a man of prayer and wrote a booklet entitled, *How to Pray.* A student once went to Dr. Torrey's office with a particular need, so they knelt in prayer. The student remarked later that Torrey had interceded vigorously and a pool of tears remained when Torrey arose.

Dr. Torrey was also an excellent Bible teacher. Dr. James M. Gray wrote: "To the church at large Dr. Torrey was known as an evangelist, and with good reason; but to some of us who were associated with him in the 80's and 90's he was always the Bible teacher. Few men were better equipped than he to expound the Holy Scriptures before a popular audience or in a classroom. . . ."

Torrey also served as dean of the Bible Institute of Los Angeles (Biola) from 1912 to 1924, and he pastored The Church of the Open Door in Los Angeles. He was author of more than forty books on salvation, soul-winning, and theology. He died on October 26, 1928, having left behind the fruit of thousands of souls, having written material to influence men for Christ, and having contributed to the furtherance of the Gospel through his leadership in Bible institutes.

## From the Sermon, "What Will the Verdict Be?"

*Ah! But that is not so solemn as it will be when you and I stand face to face with God and each one of us gives account of himself to God and God pronounces the verdict that will decide our eternity, yes, our eternity. It makes a thoughtful man shudder just to think of it! "So then every one of us shall give account of himself to God." I cannot think of anything more solemn than that, and the man who is not set to thinking by it must have a very torpid brain. You may*

try to laugh it off, and may think you are very smart in doing so. Listen, my friend, you are playing the fool. Your own best self tells you that you are playing the fool. "So then every one of us shall give account of himself to God."

# Henry Clay Morrison

## (1857–1942)

H. C. Morrison was born in Barren County, Kentucky. His parents died when he was young, and Morrison was reared in his grandfather's home. The rugged religious atmosphere and the constant spirit of revival throughout the Bluegrass Country made a profound impression upon him. It awakened within him a consciousness of his need of Christ and deliverance from sin. About the age of eleven, Morrison was converted and soon felt the call to the ministry. Although he made no attempt to preach for about eight years, Morrison occupied himself with church work. At the age of nineteen he was licensed to preach and demonstrated the validity of his call in his work as circuit rider and station pastor. As a young man he was called to one of the most responsible Methodist churches in Kentucky. In 1890 he left the pastorate and gave himself to the work of evangelism and the publication of a religious paper called *The Old Methodist,* which later became *The Herald.* Morrison's evangelistic leadership in Methodism grew rapidly from Kentucky to the other states and foreign lands. A contemporary said of him, "To him was given by God a heart to move the multitude, a mind to think God's thoughts, and a voice to rouse his century, his church, and his country." The camp meeting became one of his chief instruments, and perhaps no other man ever gave more time or effective leadership to this phase of evangelism. In addition, he served as president of Asbury College from 1910 to 1925 and from 1933 to 1940. He was instrumental in founding Asbury Theological Seminary in 1923. William Jennings Bryan said, "I regard H. C. Morrison the greatest pulpit orator on the American continent," and at Morrison's death in 1942, someone wrote of him, ". . . a tall tree has fallen in the forest, but it went down with a great shout of victory. He died as he lived . . . in the midst of a campaign for souls."

# John Wilbur Chapman

## (1859–1918)

John Chapman was born in Indiana and educated at Oberlin College and Lane Seminary. He received the LLD degree from Heidelberg University. Chapman held pastorates in Ohio, Indiana, New York, and Pennsylvania. He conducted evangelistic campaigns in Canada, Hawaii, the Fiji Islands, Australia, New Zealand, England, Scotland, Japan, Tasmania, and the Philippine Islands. Chapman became the director of the Winona Lake Bible Conference and helped establish conferences at Stony Brook, Long Island, and Montreat, North Carolina. He became executive secretary of the Presbyterian General Assembly in 1903. He was responsible for winning thousands of souls to Jesus Christ and influenced hundreds of young men to enter the ministry. He was cultured, earnest, enthusiastic and consistent. In his preaching, Chapman was never coarse or thoughtless. His preaching was calm, but forceful, emotional, but not dramatic.

## From the Sermon, "Sowing and Reaping"

*My heart grieves for any sinner who stays away from the Saviour. I have a mind to give my place on the platform to someone else, so that I might go back through the building to this one and that one, and say: Turn ye! Turn ye! For why will you die? I have a mind to lay hold upon you and compel you to come, for there is only one way in all this world to escape the law of which I am speaking. That way is this: Believe on the Lord Jesus Christ and thou shalt be saved. If thou shalt confess with thy mouth the Lord Jesus, and shalt believe in thy heart that God hath raised Him from the dead, thou shalt be saved. Can I say any more than this? God help you! Some of you are sitting there and saying to yourselves: "I am too timid." Come down when the crowd rises. Some of you are saying: "I can settle it here." It would be worth everything for you to come out in the open and walk down this aisle. Come forward and let me take your hand, and let me hear you say: "God being my helper, I am going to turn to Christ to-night." Now is the time.*

# Jonathan Goforth

## (1859–1936)

Jonathan Goforth was converted to Christ at the age of eighteen. While attending college, Goforth did rescue mission work. He read Hudson Taylor's book about missionary work in China, and it so moved him that he dedicated his life to the Lord as a missionary. He and his wife labored in Honan, China, under the China Inland Mission, training hundreds of Chinese pastors and evangelists. Goforth identified with the Chinese, even to the extent of dress and diet. His indigenous missionary work in Inland China led to a grass-roots acceptance of Goforth and the Gospel he preached. During the Boxer Rebellion of 1900 the Goforths barely escaped, although they suffered severe wounds. They returned to the Orient and were responsible for the revival in Korea in 1907. Revival seemed to follow the Goforths as they went back to China. In 1925 they went to Manchuria and served there for eight years before ill health forced them to return to Canada. Although Goforth was blind the last years of his life, he and his wife promoted missions until they went home to be with the Lord.

## From the Sermon, "Back Row Christianity"

*What would Christ have thought of His disciples had they acted in this way, and what does He think of us today as we continue to spend most of our time and money in giving the Bread of Life to those who have heard so often while millions in China are still starving? God spoke to me that night about my responsibility regarding China and I promised Him then that if He opened my way, I would when old enough go to the "back rows." Later on when other claims seemed insistent and one was tempted to care for the front rows only, the vision of China's need as I had seen it that night always came before my eyes. I could not get away from it and finally said, "Lord, here am I, send me — to the back rows."*

156

# Reuben (Uncle Bud) Robinson

## (1860–1942)

Uncle Bud Robinson was born in a log cabin in the primitive mountain region of Tennessee. When he was sixteen his father died, and his mother sold what little they had and moved to Texas. In August 1880, during a camp meeting he felt deep conviction for his sin and received Christ as his Saviour. That same night, while lying under the wagon, he felt that the Lord had called him to preach. He had no formal education, and stuttered so badly that he could hardly pronounce his name clearly. Yet in the first year of preaching he saw about three hundred conversions in his meetings. On January 10, 1893, he married Miss Sallie Harper at Georgetown, Texas. For the next two years he preached on the Hubbard Circuit. The remaining forty-seven years of his ministry were given to evangelism.

Uncle Bud had a wisdom all his own, with unusual insight into the purpose for the redeemed man here on earth — a holy walk day by day. His personal philosophy is reflected in the following request he prayed each morning: "O Lord, give me a backbone as big as a sawlog and ribs like sleepers under the church floor; put iron shoes on me and galvanized breeches and hang a wagon load of determination in the gable-end of my soul, and help me to sign the contract to fight the devil as long as I have a vision and bite him as long as I have a tooth, and then gum him till I die. Amen."

During his long ministry Uncle Bud is estimated to have traveled over two million miles, preached over thirty-three thousand sermons, was the human instrument responsible for more than one hundred thousand conversions, personally gave more than eighty-five thousand dollars in assisting young people with their Christian education, secured over fifty-three thousand subscriptions to his church paper, *The Herald of Holiness,* and wrote fourteen books that sold more than one-half million copies. God used him greatly. From Boston to Los Angeles thousands thronged to hear him, charmed by his homespun wit and his unique presentation as a preacher of the old-fashioned Gospel to the common man.

# Rodney (Gypsy) Smith

## (1860–1947)

Rodney Smith was born in a gypsy tent near Leytonstone, England. He received no formal education. His mother died from smallpox when he was young, and she was buried by lantern-light. Her last words were, "I know God will take care of my children." His father accepted Christ and then led Rodney to Christ at age fifteen. He was a stern man who would walk a mile on Saturday night for a bucket of water, rather than travel on Sunday. Two years later the young gypsy joined General William Booth's mission and began preaching to crowds that numbered from one hundred to fifteen hundred. In 1878, two years after joining Booth, Smith married Anne Pennock.

Continuing his evangelistic work, he became known as "Gypsy." He was dismissed from the Salvation Army and made the first of some thirty trips to North America in 1886. He ministered to his own people via a Gypsy Gospel Wagon Mission begun in Edinburgh in 1892. He conducted evangelistic campaigns in the United States and Scotland for over seventy years. He twice traveled around the world as an evangelist. In the Paris Opera House, he had one hundred and fifty conversions from the "cream" of Parisian society. Rodney "Gypsy" Smith died August 4, 1947, enroute to America. It is said that he never held a meeting without conversions.

## From the Sermon, "As Jesus Passed By"

*Listen — the fingers that weaved the rainbow into a scarf and wrapped it around the shoulders of the dying storm, the fingers that painted the lily-bell and threw out the planets, the fingers that were dipped in the mighty sea of eternity and shook out on this old planet, making the ocean to drop and the rivers to stream — the same fingers can take hold on these tangled lives and can make them whole again, for He came to make the crooked straight, and the rough places plain. Blessed be God, Jesus can do for Matthew what nobody else can, and He can do for you, my brother, what your friends cannot do. He can take the desire for drink out of you; He can cure the love of gambling that is eating the soul out of you; He can put out the fires of lust that are burning in your being and consuming you by inches; He can take the devil of lying out of you, the devil of cheating out of you, of fraud out of you, of hypocrisy out of you. Jesus can do what nobody else can; the preacher cannot, the Church cannot; but the Lord Jesus, who loves you, is mighty to save.*

# C. T. Studd

## (1860–1931)

C. T. Studd was the son of a wealthy Englishman, Edward Studd. The young Studd became an excellent cricket player, and at the age of nineteen was captain of the team at Eton. He attended Cambridge University from 1880 to 1883 and was converted there to Christ through the preaching of D. L. Moody. Shortly afterwards young Studd and six other students dedicated their lives and wealth to the Lord Jesus Christ and offered themselves to Hudson Taylor for work in China. They sailed to China in 1885. Studd continued to work for several years before ill health forced him and his wife to return to England, where they turned over their property to the China Inland Mission. Studd and his wife toured the world to raise funds for missions. While touring southern India he found a climate suitable for him and his wife. He served there six years, and afterward he returned to England to make plans to go to Africa. In December 1912, he left his family and went to Africa for two years in evangelistic work. He returned home for a short time and then went back to Africa for five more years. Mrs. Studd did not join him until 1928, one year before she died. Studd died in Malaga, Africa, in 1931.

## From a Pamphlet Published Just Before Studd Sailed for Africa

*If a man counts his life as of any account dear unto himself, or desires to live many years, he had better seek some softer job. But if he feels that for him the world holds no greater honors or pleasures than to fight for Christ in the firing line, except it be to die for Him in the hottest part of the field, then by all means let him come. If a man has doubts about the Holy Scriptures — which we shall give to the people as soon as may be — or insist on putting fancy interpretations upon them, he had better go elsewhere, for in the heart of Africa at least, a whole Bible, and full and simple faith therein, is of more value than the acutest intellect the world can boast. But if he is proud to be a "fool for Christ's sake" and can condescend to fight with the unnotched sword of the Spirit of God, let him come by all means. We ask the prayers of God's people for those who "go to the front," that they turn not back nor flinch in the day of battle.*

# William Bell Riley

## (1861–1947)

W. B. Riley was born in Green County, Indiana, but the family soon moved to a log cabin in Boone County, Kentucky. In 1880 he completed sufficient schooling at a normal school in Valparaiso, Indiana, to receive his teacher's certificate. After teaching in country schools he attended college in Hanover, Indiana, where he received an A.B. degree in 1885. He served several Baptist churches in Kentucky, Indiana, and Illinois, in addition to studying at the Southern Baptist Theological Seminary in Louisville, Kentucky. On March 1, 1897, he began his ministry as pastor of the First Baptist Church, Minneapolis, Minnesota, which he served for the next fifty years. A gifted orator and preacher, he championed the cause of fundamental, evangelical Christianity. He conducted large evangelistic campaigns in which thousands were saved and built up the membership of his church to more than twenty-five hundred. On more than one occasion he debated against evolution at the University of Minnesota. In 1942 he retired from the active pastorate to devote his time to Northwestern School, which he founded on October 2, 1902. The school is known for the hundreds of ministers and missionaries who are trained in its classrooms. Dr. Riley authored at least sixty volumes, numerous booklets, and sermons in pamphlet form.

## From the Sermon, "Christianity or Communism"

*For the last few years now, the atheists of the country have been attempting to get every reference to God and every sentiment of Christianity out of government documents. They would have "In God We Trust" taken from our coin. They would have the Christian Sabbath abolished. They would put an end to the Young Men's Christian Associations that are recognized and utilized in government affairs, and they would especially impose taxes upon the Christian churches, and, if possible, drive them out of existence.*

*Up to the present moment their endeavours in this direction have brought no decided result. Our coins still carry the name of our God; our Senate and House open with Christian chaplains' prayers, and our army and navy hold, as among honoured officers, this same chaplaincy. Our Sabbath abides, and though it is constantly secularized and abused, it is everywhere respected by law and regarded as a national asset.*

164

# T. T. Martin

## (1862–1939)

T. T. Martin was born in Smith County, Mississippi, April 28, 1862. Following a childhood and youth amid the extreme poverty of the postwar South, he graduated from Mississippi College, where his father both preached and taught mathematics. While preparing a career of law, Martin felt a growing impression that he must preach. After a period of intense and prayerful self-examination, he gave up his legal ambitions and devoted himself to preparing for the ministry. He graduated from the Southern Baptist Theological Seminary in Louisville, Kentucky, in 1891. While awaiting assignment for the foreign mission work, Martin was stricken with an almost fatal attack of food poisoning, and was advised by physicians that moving to Colorado was the only chance for recovery. From 1897 to 1900 Martin was pastor in Cripple Creek, preaching in nearby camps, often in the open air. Martin recovered his health and developed the unusual strength of voice that was to carry him through almost forty years of exceptionally strenuous preaching. Martin entered full-time evangelistic work in 1900, and his ministry soon became noted for its effectiveness in bringing conviction and conversion. In the early 1900's, he began to use large tents for his meetings because most of the churches could not accommodate the crowds. Soon invitations began to come from all sections of the country. In order to fill the many requests, he gathered around him a group of evangelists and musicians whose presentation of the way of salvation was clear and sound. He personally scheduled these men in organized teams throughout the country. Active until the last few months of his life, he died on May 23, 1939, and was buried at Gloster, Mississippi. On his gravestone are the dates of his birth and death and three Scripture texts which were the core of his ministry: John 3:16, Acts 16:31, and John 5:24.

# William Ashley (Billy) Sunday
## (1862–1935)

Billy Sunday was born at Ames, Iowa, as the son of a Civil War soldier, on November 19, 1862. Because his father died when he was less than a year old, he was raised in an orphanage. His young days were hard, working in a hotel and later for Colonel John Scott. During high school young Sunday worked as a janitor. In 1883 he joined the "White Sox," becoming a professional baseball player. He was converted to Christ in 1886 through the street preaching of Harry Monroe of the Pacific Garden Mission in Chicago.

Sunday gave up his baseball career in March, 1891, and became an assistant YMCA secretary. After three years of work at the YMCA and acting as assistant to the evangelist, Reverend Dr. J. Wilbur Chapman, Sunday began preaching in his own services. He was ordained to the ministry in 1903 by the Presbytery of Chicago. Sunday preached in the army camps during World War I and later held city-wide meetings in the various cities across America. He refused to accept the invitations offered him to go abroad. In Philadelphia, over 2,300,000 people attended his crusade during a period of eight weeks. Sunday held campaigns for over twenty years and literally "burned out for Christ." At the close of each service throngs of people came forward and grasped Sunday's hand thus testifying to their conversion. Such action was called "hitting the sawdust trail" because the tabernacle floors were covered with sawdust. Sunday was noted for acrobatic feats on the platform as he preached.

The worst ever said of him was that he occasionally let his humor run wild; the best ever said of him was that he reached a million lives for Christ — the drunken, the down-and-outer, the homeless, the common man. His blazing-fisted bare-handed evangelism lives in American history.

Sunday was probably a factor in preparing the country for the passage of the 18th Amendment, and a not uncritical observer concedes that "he greatly aided the cause of temperance." Sunday died in Chicago, November 6, 1935. Services were held in Moody Memorial Church, Chicago, with 4,400 present.

## From *The Real Billy Sunday* by Elijah Brown

*Two farmers in Iowa are talking at a crossroads blacksmith shop:*
*"See here, Jones; there never was any preachin' done jes' like that baseball man does it. I tell you, John, he's got more life in him than any two-year-old-colt you ever saw. I would never 'a' believed it if I hadn't seen it, that anybody could ever be so much in airnest at jes' preachin'. He's got a platform to stand on more'n as big as two wagon boxes, and he kivers every inch of it in every sermon he preaches. Why, in the meetin' last Sunday he got so fired up that he tore off both his vest and coat, jerked off his collar an' kervat, an' then rolled up his sleeves as if he was a-goin' to help thrash. My, how he does wake folks up, an' keep 'em on tenterhooks! Go to sleep? Well, I should say not! Not under the preachin' that's done in that tent. Why, John, he pounds his p'ints clear through you, and makes 'em stick out on the other side. I thought I'd been a-hearin' ruther strong preachin' all my life, but I never heard none that took hold of me like his'n does."*

## From the Sermon, "Booze"

*When you come staggering home, cussing right and left and spew-*

### William Ashley Sunday

ing and spitting, your wife suffers, your children suffer. Don't think
that you are the only one that suffers. A man that goes to the
penitentiary makes his wife and children suffer just as much as he
does. You're placing a shame on your wife and children. If you're
a dirty, low-down, filthy, drunken, whisky-soaked bum you'll affect
all with whom you come in contact. If you're a God-fearing man
you will influence all with whom you come in contact. You can't live
by yourself.

I occasionally hear a man say, "It's nobody's business how I live."
Then I say he is the most dirty, low-down, whisky-soaked, beer-
guzzling, bull-necked, foul-mouthed hypocrite that ever had a brain
rotten enough to conceive such a statement and lips vile enough to
utter it. You say, "If I am satisfied with my life why do you want to
interfere with my business?"

If I heard a man beating his wife and heard her shrieks and the
children's cries and my wife would tell me to go and see what was the
matter, and I went in and found a great, big, broad-shouldered,
whisky-soaked, hog-jowled, weasel-eyed brute dragging a little woman
around by the hair, and two children in the corner unconscious from
his kicks and the others yelling in abject terror, and he said, "What
are you coming in to interfere with my personal liberty for? Isn't
this my wife, didn't I pay for the license to wed her?" You ought, or
you're a bigamist. "Aren't these my children; didn't I pay the doctor
to bring them into the world?" You ought to, or you're a thief. "If I
want to beat them, what is that your business, aren't they mine?"
Would I apologize? Never! I'd knock seven kinds of pork out of
that old hog.

170

# George Campbell Morgan

## (1863–1945)

George Campbell Morgan was born in Tetbury, England. His home was such that he wrote, "While my father could not compel me to be a Christian, I had no choice because of what he did for me and what I saw in him." At the age of twelve he was preaching regularly in country chapels during his Sundays and holidays. In 1886 at the age of twenty-three, he left the teaching profession for which he had been trained and began devoting his full time to a teaching ministry of the Word of God. His reputation as a preacher and Bible expositor soon encompassed England and spread to the United States. The many thousands of converts from the ministry of D. L. Moody needed a teacher of the Bible to strengthen their faith. G. Campbell Morgan went to the United States and became that teacher. After five very successful years, he returned to England in 1904 and became the pastor of Westminster Chapel, London. His preaching and his weekly Friday night Bible classes were attended by thousands. Leaving Westminster Chapel in 1919, he once again returned to the United States where he conducted an itinerant ministry for fourteen years. Finally in 1933 he returned to England to again become pastor of Westminster Chapel until his retirement in 1943. He died on May 16, 1945. His paramount contribution lay in teaching the Bible and showing people how to study the Scripture for themselves.

## From G. Campbell Morgan, The Man and His Ministry

*At the age of nineteen my early faith passed under eclipse, and I ceased to preach, which I had begun to do at the age of thirteen. For two years my Bible was shut; two years of sadness and sorrow. Strange, alluring, materialistic theories were in the air, and to these I turned. . . . In my despair I took all the books I had, placed them in a cupboard, turned the key, and there they remained for seven years. I bought a new Bible and began to read it with an open mind and a determined will. That Bible found me. The Book gave forth a glow which warmed my heart, and the Word of God which I read therein gave to my troubled soul the relief and satisfaction that I had sought for elsewhere. Since that time I have lived for one end — to preach the teachings of the Book that found me.*

172

# John Hyde

## (1865–1912)

John Hyde, better known as "Praying Hyde" was born in Carrollton, Illinois. His father was a Presbyterian minister who faithfully proclaimed the Gospel message and continually prayed to the Lord to thrust out laborers into the harvest. His father prayed this not only in the pulpit but also in the home at the family altar. An indelible impression was made on young John as he grew up in this atmosphere. John graduated from Carthage College with high honors and was immediately elected to a position on the faculty. However, he had a divine call to the regions beyond, so he resigned his faculty position and entered the Presbyterian Seminary in Chicago. He graduated in the spring of 1892 and sailed for India the following October. His ministry of prayer in India during the next twenty years was so well known that the natives referred to him as "the man who never sleeps." Also, he was called the "Apostle of Prayer," but more familiarly he was known as "Praying Hyde." John Hyde was all these and more, for deep in India he sought the Lord, and the strength of meeting his Master face to face prepared him for missionary service. Often he spent thirty days and nights in prayer and many times was on his knees in deep intercession for thirty-six hours at a time. His work among the villages was so successful that for years he led four to ten people a day to the Lord Jesus Christ. Hyde was instrumental in establishing the annual Sialkot Conferences, from which thousands of missionaries and native workers returned to their stations with new power for the work of reaching India with the Gospel. Hyde's life of sacrifice, humility, love for souls and deep spirituality, as well as his example in the ministry of intercession, inspired many to follow his example in their own lives and ministries. He died February 17, 1912. His last words were: "Shout the victory of Jesus Christ."

# William Edward Biederwolf

## (1867–1939)

William Beiderwolf was converted to Christ at the age of twenty. After extensive education at universities in France, Germany, and Princeton, he was ordained at thirty years of age. He spent three years in the pastorate and one year as an army chaplain, and then began a life of evangelistic work that lasted thirty-five years. He preached in America and around the world, establishing a leper home in Korea in 1920. In 1923 he established the Winona Lake Assembly, Winona Lake, Indiana. After his active work in evangelism, he devoted his remaining years to pastoring and writing. He was the author of numerous books, among which were *The Millennium Bible*, *The Wonderful Christ*, and *The Growing Christian*.

## From a Sermon, "Frozen Assets"

*What a blessing to this old, stricken and needy world the many merchant-princes, the creators of vast wealth, have been who have refused to horde their riches; Colgate, the soap man; Hyde, the mentholatum man; Crowell, the Quaker Oats man; Kraft, the Cheese man; Tom Smith, the Apple king, and Sidney Smith, the Grain merchant, and a host of others like them who have laid whole fortunes on the altar of philanthropy!*

*Oh, the "Frozen Assets" of the Church of the living God! Think of the vast stores of wealth, of ability to serve, of personality and of power in the great army of men and women who compose her membership. Then think of the great need of this sad and troubled world. If but a fraction of this stored up potentiality could be released in sacrificial service for the cause of Christ, what a transformation in things pertaining to the kingdom of God the eyes of this present generation would behold.*

*May there be a searching of lives here this morning, and in so far as we must honestly admit that we have "frozen assets" of our own, let us ask the Holy Spirit of God to warm our hearts until they become "liquid" for service in the name of Christ.*

*Yes, it is true, indeed, the life that counts is the life that serves.*

# George W. Truett

## (1867–1944)

George W. Truett was born on May 6, 1867, at Hayesville, Clay County, North Carolina. He was converted to Christ at the age of nineteen and surrendered his will to God for service. In 1890 he was ordained into the Gospel ministry. In 1897 he graduated from Baylor University and in September of that year was called to the pastorate of the First Baptist Church, Dallas, Texas, remaining there for forty-seven years. Under his leadership the First Baptist Church grew into the largest church in the world at the time. Dr. Truett served as president of the Southern Baptist Convention from 1927-1929 and as president of the Baptist World Alliance from 1934-1939. He was one of America's greatest preachers. He always preached for a decision. He authored many books and maintained correspondence to the unsaved two mornings each week. Under his ministry there were 18,124 additions to the church; 5,337 baptisms; 4,000 in Sunday School. He went to be with the Lord on July 7, 1944, at Dallas, Texas.

## From the Sermon,
## "The Privilege and Peril of Opportunity"

*You are your brother's keeper, and if you ignore the brother the blood of that brother will cry unto God against you. Ignore the world's need, and the world's darkness, and the world's sickness, and the world's wounds, and the world's sin, and God will somehow carry forward His purposes; but retribution appalling will come to you. Your education is not given you that you may get off into some corner and chatter in polysyllables that people may say how smart you are. Your education is given you that you may fling off your coat and get into the big battle of life, to help the weak and needy and downtrodden, the ignorant and the beaten on the roadside, to help them up and on to happiness and noblest serviceableness. Your money is not given you that you may loll and dress and dawdle. The world needs it, and woe betide those who forget what money is for! The meaning of all opportunity always is service. It is not enough for a man to be clever. It is not enough for a man to be smart. It is not enough for a man to be a scholar. It is not enough for a man to be a moneymaker. The meaning of all strength is to serve the world. The correct life principle for all mankind is Paul's principle of debtorship to all. All power is under inexorable bonds to serve humanity.*

# William Reed Newell

## (1868–1956)

Born on May 22, 1868, William Reed Newell, American Bible teacher and pastor, attended Wooster College in Ohio, graduating in 1891. After studies at Princeton and Oberlin Seminaries, he pastored the Bethesda Congregational Church in Chicago until 1895. At this time Moody invited him to become the Assistant Superintendent of Moody Bible Institute under R. A. Torrey. In this position Newell demonstrated his extraordinary gift of Bible exposition. Great audiences in Chicago, St. Louis, and Toronto flocked to hear his city-wide Bible classes. This led to the publication of his well-known commentaries, especially: *Romans, Verse-By-Verse; Hebrews, Verse-By-Verse;* and *The Book of Revelation.* During this period Newell wrote the beloved Gospel hymn, "At Calvary." He was called into the presence of his Lord on April 1, 1956. Few men have had a clearer grasp of the magnitude of God's grace in Christ, and few have been able to convey it with such lasting results.

## Newell's Prayer to Understand the Scripture

*O God, the God and Father of our Lord Jesus Christ, Who in infinite love and condescension hast given us by Thy Holy Spirit that blessed Book we call The Bible, help us, we beseech Thee, as we study it! We do not, we dare not, come to the Bible merely to increase our knowledge, but to learn Thy will. We are creatures of Thy hand. "Thou art the God in Whose hand our breath is, and Whose are all our ways." Humbly we beseech Thee, in the name of our Lord Jesus Christ, grant us grace to fear and love Thee truly. Bring us into a godly life.*

*May the Holy Spirit whom Thou hast sent to open to us this Bible which He inspired, truly enlighten us, teach us, and lead us to glorify Thee in this brief life, before we meet Thee face to face!*

*All this we humbly ask in the name of Thy dear Son, Jesus Christ our Lord and Saviour. Amen.*

# Lee Rutland Scarborough

## (1870–1945)

L. R. Scarborough was born in Colfax, Louisiana, on July 4, 1870, one of five children. Lee was converted to Christ at seventeen. After graduating from Baylor University in 1892, he taught at that institution for the next two years. Then he entered Yale University, where he received an additional degree in 1896. Upon completion of his seminary work at Southern Baptist Theological Seminary in Louisville, Kentucky, in 1900, Scarborough pastored in Texas for the next eight years. In 1908 he went to Southwestern Baptist Theological Seminary in Fort Worth, Texas, as a professor in the School of Theology, a post he held until he was elected president of the seminary in 1915. He served in that capacity for the next twenty-seven years, until he retired in 1942. During this period he also served as president of the Baptist General Convention of Texas (1929-31); vice-president of the Southern Baptist Convention (1934-35); president of the Southern Baptist Convention (1938-41); and vice-president of the Baptist World Alliance (1940-41). Dr. Scarborough was the author of fourteen books, as well as a great preacher and soul winner. He died in Amarillo, Texas, on April 10, 1945.

## From the Sermon, "The Tears of Jesus"

*He looked me in the face and said, "I am 60 years of age and for thirty years I have been not only an infidel but an atheist. I do not believe in Jesus Christ. I neither believe that He was the Son of God, nor the Son of Mary. I believe the whole story is the product of an inflamed imagination and that there was no such person as Jesus Christ." . . . I looked into his face. The tears were coming down his cheeks. I said, "You do not believe in God. You do not believe in the Bible. Do you believe that you are a sinner?" And, with a trembling voice, he said, "I know I am a sinner." "Then," I said, "my friend, I know I have a Savior. Let's pray." . . . I had not finished the prayer until he leaped from his knees and said, "I have found Him and He is mine. I deny the denials of thirty years. Jesus Christ is real to me." . . . I have come from that incident remembering that unsaved men are helpless men and that somebody must bring them to Jesus Christ.*

# Melvin Ernest Trotter

## (1870–1940)

Mel Trotter was born in Orangeville, Illinois, as the son of a godly mother and a drunken father. His mother tried to teach him to pray, but he followed the footsteps of his father and became a drunkard. He left home at the age of seventeen, but the prayers of a faithful mother followed him constantly. After years of drink and sin, and on the verge of self-destruction, Mel ventured into the Pacific Garden Mission in Chicago where he heard the Gospel. That night he responded to the invitation to receive Christ as his Saviour, and his life was transformed. Pacific Garden Mission was responsible for the social and spiritual salvation of a number of men on "skid row" and Trotter never forgot the impact the mission made on his life. Later he entered the ministry and was ordained a Presbyterian minister. After conducting some evangelistic meetings he was called to be superintendent of a rescue mission in Grand Rapids, Michigan. He preached with pathos in his voice and frequently gave his testimony of the deliverance that came only through the power of God. Those who knew Trotter testified that thousands of "drunks and winos" were dried out and given purpose and stability in life through the influence of Trotter. Still, thousands more, who never tasted drink nor were on "skid row," were reached for salvation through his preaching in churches and evangelistic crusades. His unusual burden for the spiritual needs of the "down and out" prompted him to establish sixty-seven rescue missions from Boston to San Francisco. America will long remember Mel Trotter as the "Bishop of the Bowery" and the preacher who never forgot the habit from which he was delivered. He was known as the man who "raved about Jesus."

# Lewis Sperry Chafer

## (1871–1952)

Lewis Sperry Chafer, Bible lecturer and theologian, was born on February 27, 1871, at Rock Creek, Ohio. He graduated from Oberlin College in 1892 and was ordained to the Presbyterian ministry in 1900. Chafer launched into evangelism, demonstrating talent as a Gospel singer and preacher. He toured as a renowned Bible lecturer from 1914 until 1924. While conducting this active ministry, he became burdened for young men entering the ministry. He recognized the need for a preparation that emphasized expository preaching and teaching of the Bible. He contacted other noted Bible scholars and shared his concern with them. As a result of his vision, classes began at Dallas Theological Seminary in the fall of 1924, with Chafer as president. He remained in that office till his death. He wrote many books, including his monumental eight-volume *Systematic Theology*. His students remember best his deep reverence for the Word, and a daily, humble dependence on the Holy Spirit. Dr. Chafer died on August 22, 1952, but his work continues through his books and his students. Thousands of individuals gained new spiritual understanding and power from reading his books. Each book has become a standard work in its field.

## From *Systematic Theology, Volume I*

. . . *Primarily, the theologian is appointed to systematize the truth contained in the Bible and to view it as the divinely inspired Word which God has addressed to man. Therefore, such investigations as men may conduct in the field of proof or disproof that the Bible is God's inerrant message to man are, for the most part, extratheological and to be classified as pertaining to Biblical criticism rather than Systematic Theology. . . . Systematic Theology designs to construct a science or order out of the Biblical revelation and on the basis that it is ὁ λόγος τοῦ Θεοῦ ("the Word of God"), and, as surgery must proceed on the basis of belief in the existence of the mortal body, so, and in like manner, Systematic Theology must proceed on the basis of the belief that the Bible is, in all its parts, God's own Word to man.*

# Thomas Todhunter Shields

## (1873–1955)

T. T. Shields was born in Bristol, England. At an early age he was converted to Christ during a revival meeting in his father's church. He was educated in British universities. After a few pastorates in England he was called to the Jarvis Street Baptist Church in Toronto, Canada, in 1910. Here he served for forty-five years. However, his service for Christ was not confined to the Jarvis Street Church. He was very active in several areas: Vice-chairman of the Home Mission Board of the Baptist Convention of Ontario and Quebec, President of the Baptist Union of North America, Vice-President of the International Council of Christian Churches, President of the Union of Regular Baptist Churches of Ontario and Quebec, President of the Conservative Baptist Churches of Canada, President of the Canadian Council of Evangelical Christian Churches, and President of the Canadian Protestant League. In 1927 Dr. Shields organized the Toronto Baptist Seminary. He also was the author of a number of Christian books. Because he was the leading exponent of fundamental Christianity in Canada, he became known as the "Spurgeon of Canada."

## From the Sermon, "The Exclusiveness of Faith"

*. . . That is merely making use of God in cases of emergency. God becomes very much like those tools you see in the railway car, painted red, behind a glass, with no hinges, and then on the glass is written: "For use in cases of emergency only." When you are hard up you have got to the end of yourself, you have done the best you could, and you can do no more, then you will ask God to do the little that remains, to save you from default by supplementing your own efforts. That is not faith. . . .*

*So do we think of God. So do we cherish our pride, and our self-sufficiency, determined to have some part. Blessed is the man who knows his own bankruptcy, and knows he has reached the end of all his resources, and exhorts his soul: "My soul, wait thou only upon God; for my expectation is from him." In so far as I have any part in it at all, it will only be because His grace and energy enable me to do certain things, for of myself I can do nothing at all. That is what it means to believe God: God or nothing: God or defeat, God or rain. Yes; God or eternal damnation. "My soul, wait thou only upon God."*

# Louis Entzminger

## (1876–1958)

Louis Entzminger began his service for the Lord with a great desire to work with the Sunday schools of Baptist churches. Dr. J. Frank Norris gathered great crowds and registered numerous conversions at the First Baptist Church of Fort Worth, Texas. When Dr. Norris saw the difficulty of conserving the results of his evangelism, he sent the following telegram to Entzminger on July 9, 1913, "Will you consider coming as the superintendent of the First Baptist Church Sunday School in Fort Worth to build the largest Sunday School in the world . . .?" Entzminger came and is credited with doing just that — a Sunday school with an average weekly attendance of 5,500. He divided the multitudes into small classes for Bible instruction and substituted a "Bible only" curriculum in place of the then accepted International Uniform Lesson. Entzminger originated the six-point system widely used today in Baptist Sunday schools and other denominations. Dr. Entzminger was known for the great Sunday school crusades he held in the United States and Canada. Some of the largest Sunday schools look back to a crusade with Dr. Entzminger that began their spectacular growth. He was instrumental in the founding of the Fundamental Baptist Bible Institute, which later became the Bible Baptist Seminary in Arlington, Texas. After more than eighty years of life, the majority of them in full-time service for the Lord, Dr. Entzminger slipped quietly away to be with the Lord. His life could well be summed up in the words of another: "Life's race well won, life's work well done, life's crown well won, now, comes rest!"

# Harry A. Ironside

## (1876–1951)

At the age of twelve, H. A. Ironside heard Dwight L. Moody preach, and received Christ two years later. He described his conversion, "I rested on the Word of God and confessed Christ as my Saviour." From that moment the Word of God seemed to be like a burning fire in his bones, and he gave his first public testimony three nights later at a Salvation Army meeting. Shortly afterwards Ironside began preaching and became known as "the boy preacher of Los Angeles." Although he had little formal education, his tremendous mental capacity and photographic memory caused him to be called the "Archbishop of Fundamentalism." A prolific writer, he contributed regularly to various religious periodicals and journals in addition to publishing over eighty books and pamphlets. His writings included addresses or commentaries on the entire New Testament, all of the prophetic books of the Old Testament, and a great many volumes on specific Bible themes and subjects. For eighteen of his fifty years of ministry, he was pastor of the Moody Memorial Church in Chicago. He went to be with the Lord on January 16, 1951, while on a preaching tour in New Zealand.

## From the Sermon, "Divine Priorities"

*What is the real trouble in our country today? Is it not just this, that we have not given God His rightful place in our national life, and so His chastening rod is upon us? We have put money-making and pleasure-seeking first. We have said, "I want to live my own life," and the result has been ruin and disaster. Oh, for a national return to God and His Word, a recognition of the divine priorities!*

*Put first things first in your life. Give God the priority in your home, in connection with your talents, your service, everything that occupies you. If you thus seek Him first, He guarantees to stand back of you and never let you fall. Recognize the divine priorities and you will enter into a life of blessing such as you have never known before.*

192

# John Franklyn Norris

## (1877–1952)

John Franklyn Norris was born in Dadeville, Alabama, 1877, but spent his childhood and youth in Hubbard, Texas, where the crusading spirit of the old West gave him life's direction. As a boy he was shot three times when horse thieves were attacking his father because he testified against the gang. Mrs. Norris knew her son was going to live and be a preacher, even though the doctors gave him up to die. He graduated from Baylor University, and was valedictorian of his class at the Southern Baptist Theological Seminary in Louisville, Kentucky. He was ordained to the ministry in 1899 and soon thereafter began his long stormy career by serving as editor of "The Baptist Standard." He crusaded against the liquor traffic and horse racing, leading to passage of new laws in Texas. Norris aided Dr. B. H. Carroll in the founding of Southwestern Baptist Theological Seminary in Forth Worth, Texas.

In 1909 he accepted the pastorate of the First Baptist Church of Fort Worth, Texas, and remained there until his death. Norris continued his crusade against corruption in city politics. Twice his church was burned to the ground, but he rebuilt it. An unruly mob gathered on a Ft. Worth street and an agitator offered $1,000 to the person who would shoot J. Frank Norris. Upon hearing about the mob, Norris went to the street corner and, in view of the crowd, bought a newspaper and turned to read it leaving his back as a target. On another occasion a crowd gathered in the town hall and threatened to hang Norris. He strolled into the meeting and sat in the first row. The dynamic preaching of Norris gave him the reputation of being able to draw a crowd of 5,000 to 10,000 any place in Texas.

In 1935 Norris also accepted the pastorate of Temple Baptist Church, Detroit, Michigan, and held joint pastorates for fifteen years of these two great churches, separated geographically by thirteen hundred miles. During those years the attendance of each Sunday school reached over 5,000 weekly under the leadership of one pastor, and constituted the world's largest Sunday schools. His newspapers, *The Fundamentalist* and *The Searchlight,* claimed to have the largest circulation of a religious newspaper west of the Mississippi. A master pulpiteer, Dr. Norris was a fierce opponent of Communism, Catholicism, liberalism, and evolution and was acclaimed to be one of the twentieth century's outstanding leaders of Bible fundamentalism. In 1939, with the aid of Dr. Louis Entzminger, he organized the Bible Baptist Seminary in Fort Worth, Texas, an institution which excelled in the training of young preachers. Many of the graduates of this school have built some of the largest churches in America.

Norris was a personal friend of world leaders such as William Jennings Bryan, Winston Churchill, and Franklin Roosevelt. He preached to state legislators and is credited with personally swinging the Texas vote from Al Smith, the Catholic candidate, to Herbert Hoover in 1928.

A friend of world leaders, compassionate soul winner, and Bible expositor, Dr. Norris died in Keystone, Florida, August 20, 1952, and was buried in Fort Worth, Texas, Saturday, August 24, 1952.

## From the Sermon,
## "Twenty-four Truths Set Forth in Baptism"

*First, every time a believer is baptized he declares his faith in the authority of our Lord and Saviour, Jesus Christ. He came and said, "All power," and the word power there means authority, "is given unto me in heaven and in earth."*

*Then, after "teaching" he said, "baptizing them." On what basis; on what authority? . . .*

*The Rationalists say, "We go by reason. There is no such thing as revelation."*

*Our Romanist friends say, "We believe in the infallibility of the papacy. And everything is interpreted in the light of that decree."*

*We come back and answer, "Not in a man's reason; not in some ecclesiastical power, but in the Word of God. What is revealed in the law and the testimony? What do they say?" Therefore, every time that we baptize we acknowledge Him as our Supreme authority.*

*Second, Baptism Declares We Have a New Captain*

*One of the finest illustrations of that is what Paul said in I Cor. 10:1-2, "Moreover, brethren, I would not that ye should be ignorant, how that all our fathers were under the cloud, and all passed through the sea." Remember that the sea divided. Two walls on either side, and the cloud overshadowed them. They were immersed. And by that dividing of the sea, overshadowed by the cloud, they said this,*

195

# John Franklin Norris

*"We are now coming under a new leadership. The tyranny of Pharaoh is through. We have left Egypt. We are on our way to Canaan's fair and happy land."*

*Therefore, as we come into baptism that means we no longer are led captive by his will, the devil, but we have a new Captain.*

*Third, baptism is a commandment. And every time we are baptized we say to the world, "I'm obeying His command where Peter said, 'Repent and be baptized every one of you.'"*

*Fourth, baptism declares the New Birth. "Then they that gladly received his word were baptized." And receiving His word is the human side of "Ye must be born again."*

*Fifth, Baptism declares our faith in the Divine Trinity. And every time that a believer is baptized he says to the world, "I am not a Unitarian. I believe in the triune God." Therefore we are baptized "in the name of the Father and of the Son and of the Holy Ghost."*

*Sixth, Baptism declares the Fatherhood of God. Oh, what an error — "the Father of all men." God is our Father save and only through faith in Jesus Christ. And there is not a worse error that has crept into this world, than to say that all people are children of God. We are made children of God by faith in Jesus Christ, and that is how the family of heaven is made up.*

*Seventh, Baptism declares the Sonship of Jesus. We are baptized in the name of the Son. And that means in His authority; in His likeness; and we accept His word and we follow Him.*

*Eighth, Baptism declares the work of the Holy Spirit. Therefore, in the name of the Holy Spirit by which we are regenerated born of the Spirit, not of the flesh. It is by the Spirit of God that He offered Himself on the cross. The first mention of the Holy Spirit is in the second verse of the first chapter of the Bible, "And the Spirit of God moved upon the face of the deep." And in these first three verses you will find the whole plan of salvation. Creation perfect; creation imperfect; creation made again. That is exactly the state of man — created in innocence; second, failure and sin; third, made a new creation in Christ Jesus. That tells us how that sin and righteousness met on the cross; that tells us how that justice and mercy met on the cross; that tells us how that all of heaven and all of hell met on the cross; that tells us how that time and eternity met on the cross. Therefore, God was in Christ.*

196

# William Graham Scroggie

## (1877–1958)

William Graham Scroggie was born at Great Malvern, England, of Scottish parents. He was one of nine children in a home without normal educational advantages. He grew up among the brethren, and after a few years in business he entered Spurgeon's College in London at the age of nineteen to train for the Baptist ministry. He was turned out of his first two churches in London and Yorkshire because of his opposition to modernism and worldliness. Scroggie began to study the Bible; and during the next two difficult years, when he lived with little support, he laid the foundation of all his subsequent work. After pastorates in England, Scotland, New Zealand, Australia, Tasmania, the United States, and Canada, he became pastor of the famous Spurgeon Metropolitan Tabernacle, London. During World War II his home was bombed on three occasions, and his historic church building destroyed during an air raid. Increasing ill health forced him to retire in 1944. He devoted his remaining years to completing his literary work, *The Unfolding Drama of Redemption*. He died on December 28, 1958.

## From the Sermon, "The Being of God"

*. . . God does not visit men in judgment for the neglect of that of which they had no knowledge. God was patient with men in times of darkness, for the full light had not risen. The times of their ignorance God overlooked. But now He commandeth all men everywhere to repent, because He hath appointed a day in which He will judge the world by that Man whom He hath ordained. There is the sweep of the ages. He looks behind and abroad, and He looks on. And He sees that through the ages there is one increasing purpose, and it is a redeeming purpose. That is the true philosophy of history. We have nothing like it in the world of literature. Did Paul make a mistake? We talk quite a lot about Jesus Christ, but less about the Holy Spirit, and still less about God. The other day I was asked to draw up a statement of belief for a body that was proposing to come into existence and to function in a certain way. And in this statement of belief reference was made to God the Father, to the real humanity of Jesus and to His proper Deity, and to the saving and sanctifying ministry of the Holy Spirit. And when it was read this was said to me: "Why make any reference to God the Father?" Well Why? Who is Jesus? We do not know Christ by knowing God. We know God by knowing Christ. Do we want to know what God is like? Look at Jesus Christ. . . .*

198

# Mordecai Ham

## (1878–1959)

More than 33,000 conversions were reported during the first year of evangelist Mordecai Ham's ministry. As a result of his city-wide crusades and evangelistic crusades in churches, more than 300,000 new converts joined Baptist churches in Georgia, Alabama, Mississippi, Tennessee, Kentucky, and the Carolinas in a period of thirty years. The author of the ammendment for prohibition stated that Billy Sunday and Mordecai Ham had nearly put the saloons out of business. A close observer wrote concerning him: "He exalts Christ and fights sin with all his might . . . there is no middle ground in his campaigns. Under his preaching I have seen murderers saved, drunkards converted, homes re-united, and men and women dedicate their lives for special service." Billy Graham was converted under Mordecai Ham's preaching.

## From *Billy Graham*\*

*Billy Graham, at the time, was seventeen. An old-style, hell-and-damnation evangelist, Mordecai Ham by name, had opened a three-month assault on sin in the Graham home town of Charlotte, North Carolina. There was nothing notably sinful about Billy. He was a high-school baseball and basketball star, popular with the girls. He had no very definite idea what he wanted to do with himself unless, as he sometimes hoped, he could make the major leagues as a first baseman. He was the well-thought-of, nonsmoking, nondrinking, churchgoing son of devout parents.*

*For the first several weeks, Ham's assault on sin in Charlotte left him untouched, since, despite some not-too-subtle hints from his parents, he kept himself out of reach. When one night he finally went out to the revival tent it was with a group of his high-school friends whose ideas on what else to do in Charlotte on a midsummer night had run out.*

*What he saw amazed him and, no doubt, stirred his imagination: the size of the crowd — more than 5,000, filling every seat, filling the bare-planked wooden platform, sitting on chairs, benches, and boxes beyond the tent walls; the long, sawdust-carpeted aisles; the unpainted pulpit; the "great choir," the women in white dresses, the men in shirt sleeves; most of all the scene when choir and congregation stood and sang together — basses and altos coming in with a booming volume on the chorus downbeat. . . .*

*The next night, with another friend, Grady Wilson, he sat in the choir where, though unable to carry a tune, he figured he could escape the evangelist by being behind him. The evangelist's first*

*words were: "There's a great sinner in this place tonight." Billy at once concluded: "Mother's been telling him about me." That night, when the invitation was given, Billy turned to Grady and said what thousands since have said in Billy Graham Crusades, "Let's go."*

*Billy Graham, by Stanley High, (New York: McGraw Hill Book Co., 1956), p. 34-36. Used with permission.

# Evan Roberts

## (1878–1950)

Evan Roberts, leader of the Welsh revival, worked in coal mines, but he walked in the heavenlies. Never without his Bible, he prayed and wept eleven years for revival in Wales. He entered the preparatory school for the ministry at Newcastle Emlyn when about twenty-six. He never finished. Compelled by the Holy Spirit, he returned to his home village of Loughor to tell of Christ in November, 1904, and fire fell. Evan did not preach; he led the meetings, praying, "Plyg ni, O Arglwydd!" – "Bend us, O Lord," and urging, "Obey the Holy Spirit . . . obey!" The Calvinistic Methodist church was so changed that all Loughor became a praying, praising multitude. Taverns were emptied, brothels were closed, and the churches were filled. The workmen gathered in the churches daily for prayer and confession before going to the coal mines. This spiritual fire spread until most of Wales turned to Jesus Christ in repentance and faith. Roberts burned himself out through extended prayer and ministry in the short months of the 1904-05 Welsh revival. Of all the great men to live, none ministered such a short time, yet had such a lasting influence on a nation and over such a wide population. Roberts' influence was spread throughout all the world as revival spread to other countries.

Broken in health, he retired from public view for the remaining half century of his life. Yet, he was sought for counsel by those in prominent religious circles as well as the common laborer. All loved and respected Evan Roberts because they realized at one time in his life he was a channel through whom the fires of revival burned brightly. He died quietly in his sleep.

# Paul Rader

## (1879–1938)

Paul Rader, American evangelist and pastor, was born in Denver, Colorado, the son of a Methodist minister. He was converted to Christ as a boy and became a soloist in his father's meetings. Rader was educated at the University of Denver, the University of Colorado, and did post-graduate study at Harvard University. During this time in college he drifted into liberalism and entered a business partnership, thinking little of God or of serving the Lord. While walking near Times Square in New York City, God spoke to him through an illuminated sign. Rader sought a place to pray amid the busy crowd of New York City, rented a room at a nearby hotel, and fell on his face before the Lord, dedicating his life to God. The incident transformed his life and he spoke of it many times in his future preaching. He left the business world and entered the ministry. His pastorates included a Congregational church in Boston; Christian and Missionary Alliance Tabernacle in Pittsburgh (1912-15); Moody Memorial Church in Chicago (1915-21); Chicago Gospel Tabernacle (1922-33); and Gospel Temple in Fort Wayne, Indiana (1936-37).

Rader's ministry was not characterized by the conventional American pulpit. He built huge tabernacles and his dynamic preaching attracted the crowds. The best speakers of the day were invited to the tabernacles and large services were held on Sunday afternoons and evenings to attract those from other churches. Usually, no membership was involved and little church organization was promoted. Great preaching was the catalyst of Rader's ministry. In a day when the industrial cities of the North were attracting emigrants from Europe and the poor of the South, Rader became a "minister to the rootless," and their search for meaning in life was ended in the dynamic preaching of Rader. Rader served as president of the Christian and Missionary Alliance from 1921-1923. His radio broadcasts were heard on various Chicago stations as well as the CBS Network. He was instrumental in sending scores of missionaries to countries all over the world in addition to influencing hundreds of young men to enter the ministry.

### From the Gospel Song, "Only Believe"

*Fear not little flock, from the cross to the throne*
*From death into life, he went for his own*
*All power in earth, all power above,*
*Is given to him, for the flock of His love.*
*(Chorus)*
*Only believe, only believe;*
*All things are possible only believe.*

# Ernest Ira Reveal

## (1880–1959)

Rescue mission superintendent, E. I. Reveal, the oldest of twelve children, was born in West Virginia. He left school in his teens to join his father in the contracting and bricklaying business. Gifted in this work, he prospered; however, this prosperity did not fill the void in his soul. He was converted on January 24, 1904, and soon began attending a Presbyterian church whose pastor proved to be a real friend to this new Christian. He grew rapidly in grace, entered into church activities, and was made an elder in the church. In March 1919, he was ordained a minister by the Presbytery of Indiana. His call to rescue mission work came during a convention of rescue mission workers at the Mel Trotter Mission in Grand Rapids, Michigan. Reveal learned that several pastors and laymen were interested in beginning a mission in his hometown of Evansville, Indiana. This proved to be a direct answer to prayer, for this had been on his heart for some time. From humble beginnings the rescue mission grew until the work operated not only a well-equipped modern mission in downtown Evansville, but also a summer camp outside the city. During his entire ministry, Reveal was a monument to the grace of God. Being a cripple with one leg in a strong brace did not in the least deter him from his God-given task. Living in an atmosphere of prayer and fellowship with the Heavenly Father for forty years, Reveal "prayed in" the funds that sustained and provided the means of expansion for the mission. The records of the mission show hundreds of conversions. Of these, many who are now ministers, missionaries, and laymen were brought to Christ under Reveal's ministry. As a speaker Reveal was earnest, though not eloquent, practical, though not polished, preaching the Gospel in language men of the rescue mission could understand. A deep love for Christ and a compassion for the spiritual and physical needs of the underprivileged prompted Reveal to spend much of his life in prayer.

# Robert Pierce Shuler

## (1880–1965)

Robert Shuler was born August 4, 1880, in the foothills of the Blue Ridge Mountains of Virginia. At the age of nine, kneeling between his mother and his uncle, who was the preacher in the "meetin' house" at Comer's Rock, he received Christ as his Lord and Saviour. His primary education consisted of a three-month school where he mastered the "McGuffey's Readers." In 1897 he entered Emory and Henry College as a sub-freshman and graduated in 1903. Two years later he married Nelle Reeves, and the same year he entered the Holston Conference of the Methodist Church. Endowed with a good mind and sharp wit, Shuler was an excellent extemporaneous speaker. He was in demand as an evangelistic speaker throughout the South. In addition, his great courage, coupled with his conservative theology and evangelistic fervor, prompted him to preach with the altar call in view. In 1920 he became pastor of the Trinity Methodist Church of Los Angeles, a position he occupied until his death. He began with a depleted congregation and saw it grow to five thousand members in the 1930s. The basis for growth was a dynamic pulpit ministry in which he thundered against the sin he saw around him. In 1929 he was given a radio station which was housed in the tower of his church. It became a strong voice against crime and corruption in southern California.

Shuler's church growth paralleled the growth of the population on the West Coast with its "rootless" people from all parts of America. These masses found in him a "champion of the common man," for Shuler's cry against corruption was the complaint of the masses. The politicians hated Shuler and tried every means to silence his preaching. His life was threatened, his church was bombed, he was sued and finally put in jail. He ran for United States Senator on the Prohibition Ticket in 1932 and lost by only fifty thousand votes. His writings included: *The Methodist Challenge, What New Doctrine Is This?, Some Dogs I Have Known,* and *I Met Them on the Trail.* Three of his sons followed him in the ministry.

# Walter Lewis Wilson

## (1881–1969)

Walter L. Wilson was born on May 27, 1881, in Aurora, Indiana. He was "the preacher" whenever neighborhood children played church. As a small boy he sold bark and roots on the streets of a small Arkansas town, to which his family had moved. Later, at the age of sixteen, he held evangelistic street meetings. After medical training he began to practice as a physician in Webb City, Missouri, in 1904. As a doctor, his medicine kept people from dying. As a Christian, his message pointed them to life. Everywhere he went he told people how Jesus Christ could transform their lives. His wit and charm were great assets in winning people to himself so that he could lead them to Christ. Soul-winning dominated his life, and he used every possible tool to accomplish it. A pioneer in radio, he initiated his own program in 1924. He founded, and for forty years pastored, Calvary Bible Church in Kansas City. He founded and served as president of present-day Calvary Bible College, wrote twenty-seven books, and traveled widely as a conference speaker. He died on May 24, 1969, but he lives on in the hearts of thousands who have been touched by his dynamic spiritual gifts. One could well describe him as one of this century's brightest lights in evangelical Christianity. A giant of a man, he lived everything he preached: "The blessed privilege of winning souls for Christ is most interesting, profitable, and eternally blessed."

## From "The Mystery of the Human Body," an unpublished paper

*This organ is an enigma which is unsolved. No one has ever found the time when it starts to beat. We think it is around fifteen or sixteen weeks, but no one can say definitely. We do not know whether the beat is a closing one or an opening one. We do not know how the blood, originally from the mother, enters the veins, the arteries and the heart of that tiny little unborn child. It is all a mystery. The One who made the heart is the One who equips it to operate for seventy-five years without help. He is the One who starts it and He is the One who will finish it, tell it to stop. That One who thus controls the heart wants us to give the heart to Him, and we should.*

# Robert Reynolds Jones

## (1883–1968)

Called the greatest evangelist of all time by Billy Sunday, Robert Reynolds Jones was born October 30, 1883 in Shipperville, Alabama. He was the son of William Alexander Jones, a Christian farmer of Calvinistic convictions. Dr. Bob, as he was later called, was the eleventh of twelve children. He worked hard in his youth on the farm, and his father instilled in him strong Christian convictions. Dr. Bob was something of a child prodigy when it came to preaching. He demonstrated unusual ability at memorizing Scripture and recitation. He was converted at eleven years of age, appointed a Sunday school superintendent at twelve, and ordained at fifteen by a Methodist church. He was orphaned at seventeen.

From the time of his conversion he began preaching publicly and was known as the "boy preacher." He preached to anyone who would listen. Being a good speaker and a fast thinker, he became a good debater. It was not the profoundness of his message but the straightforward manner of his presentation that touched the hearts of the people. All the essential qualities of an evangelist were his, that of strong convictions, undaunted courage, a keen imagination, dramatic ability, and sincerity. To describe his messages one might say they were relevant, to the point, and understandable. He preached to the level of the people.

When he was twenty-one, the doctor told him he had tuberculosis of the throat. He had had double pneumonia, was malaria-prone, and was told he would not live ten years. After spending some time out West, he grew stronger and completely recovered, attributing it to the healing of the Lord.

Mary Gaston Stollenwerk became his wife June 17, 1908. A woman of culture, she proved a real asset in his later years when he established Bob Jones College. Bob Jones, Jr., was born October 19, 1911. His son was destined to continue in Dr. Bob's footsteps as a great preacher and in taking charge of the college.

The man who had preached in cotton fields, brush arbors and small churches was now holding city-wide campaigns in American cities both large and small.

In 1926 Dr. Bob founded Bob Jones College (now University) in Florida near Panama City. Since then he relocated the institution at Cleveland, Tennessee, in 1933, and Greenville, South Carolina, in 1946, where the University still remains. Dr. Bob desired to combat the atheistic trend in education and build a center for Christian education. Each year more than four thousand students from every state in the union and thirty foreign countries enter this institution.

Throughout his entire ministry, Dr. Bob was a leading spokesman for the fundamental, conservative, Scriptural position, all the while opposing modernism, neo-orthodoxy, and neo-evangelicalism. He died in January, 1968. The many hundred graduates of Bob Jones University serving the Lord in churches in America and on the mission fields of the world are an extension of his ministry.

## From the Letter of Introduction,
## By-laws of Bob Jones University

*Before I founded Bob Jones University twenty-five years ago, I had had a rather wide experience as an evangelist. In my work I had met many young people whose fathers and mothers had sent them to colleges or universities which were founded as Christian schools and who had come back home from these schools with their faith shattered and some with their morals wrecked. I had learned that most of the well-known modernistic colleges and universities in America were originally built on a conservative, orthodox Christian foundation and that money had been given to these schools by consecrated Christian people because they were built on such a foundation. I knew that these schools had been wrecked spiritually because the executives and boards of trustees did not have the moral courage to discharge modernistic teachers who worshipped at the altar of a false god that they were pleased to call "academic freedom."*

*I had observed that these "academic freedom" professors had laughed the "old-time religion" out of the academic halls and had succeeded in making the impression on the minds of the masses of*

213

## Robert Reynold Jones

*young people that a person who believed in the "old-time religion" had to have a greasy nose, dirty fingernails, baggy pants, and never would shine his shoes. So I made up my mind to build a school that would stand without apology for the "old-time religion" and the absolute authority of the Bible and at the same time maintain high academic standards and put great emphasis on culture.*

*I knew very little about "standardized education." I did know, however, that there is no difference between the foundation of an individual Christian life, the foundation of a Christian home, the foundation of a Christian college, and the foundation of a Christian church. I, of course, knew that the superstructure is different; but the foundation, if it is Christ, is the same. I, therefore, made up my mind that the foundation of Bob Jones University should be an orthodox, conservative Christian foundation. So in the charter we incorporated the Bob Jones University creed and wrote in the charter that this creed could never be changed. The creed does not include all that the founder of Bob Jones University believes, but it does include all the fundamental essentials of the Christian faith which are accepted by all evangelical Christians regardless of their denominational affiliation. I had learned in my evangelistic work that it is not compromising to take a man as far as you can on the right road but that it is compromising to take a man any distance on the wrong road. Every teacher who teaches in Bob Jones University is required to sign every year the orthodox Christian creed upon which the school was founded.*

*Even the first year of the school, I learned that certain by-laws and regulations under which teachers and staff members are employed are essential to keeping an institution Christian, even though the institution does have a good orthodox foundation.*

*Some great American said, "The American people spend a good deal of time trying to find a method that will succeed; and after finding the method and succeeding they then throw away the method that gave them success."*

# William Leroy Pettingill
## (1886–1950)

Born on August 27, 1866, William Pettingill, American pastor, educator, and lecturer, received only a fourth-grade education. Although he was saved at thirteen, he did not begin serious Bible study until a decade later, after his first encounter with C. I. Scofield. From that point Pettingill moved from YMCA work into the pastorate and teaching. (Many of his twenty-one books are revised sermon studies.) In 1913 Scofield and Pettingill co-founded the Philadelphia College of the Bible, with Pettingill serving as Dean. In addition to stimulating students with his vivid visualizations of the Word and his hearty laugh, Pettingill wrote widely. He also served on the Council of the Central American Mission and was a staunch supporter of the fundamentalist movement. From 1928 to 1950 Dr. Pettingill traveled across North and Central America and to Europe, sharing his gift of stirring people to action from the Word. "Keep looking up" was his motto, and it became the challenge to many. Dr. Pettingill exchanged his faith for sight on September 15, 1950.

## From the Introduction to *Christ in the Psalms*

*Christ is the theme of the Bible (John 5:39; Heb. 10:7). He is the Word of God (John 1:1-18; Rev. 19:13), and it is the Word of God (Heb. 4:13). . . . the Word incarnate, . . . the Word written.*

*He is the theme of the whole Bible. In the New Testament not only, but in the Old Testament as well, He is the central figure. Throughout the Book, "the testimony of Jesus is the spirit of prophecy" (Rev. 19:10).*

*He Himself claimed to have been the subject of the Old Testament Scriptures when He rebuked the discouraged Emmaus disciples, saying, "O fools, and slow of heart to believe all that the prophets have spoken: ought not Christ to have suffered these things, and enter into His glory? And beginning at Moses and all the prophets, He expounded unto them in all the Scriptures the things concerning Himself" (Luke 24:25-27). To the same effect is the teaching of First Peter 1:10, 11, where it is declared that the sufferings of Christ and the glory that shall follow constitute the theme of the Old Testament writers.*

*He is, then, the theme of the Psalms. Indeed, the Psalms are especially mentioned in His words to His apostles after His resurrection: "These are the words which I spake unto you, while I was yet with you, that all things must be fulfilled, which were written in the law of Moses, and in the prophets, and in the psalms, concerning me" (Luke 24:44).*

# Charles Edward Fuller

## (1887–1968)

Charles E. Fuller was born April 25, 1887. After graduating *magna cum laude* from Pomona College, he married Grace Payton and ventured into the fruitpacking business. Fuller was converted in 1917 when he went to the Church of the Open Door in Los Angeles to hear Paul Rader preach. The next year the Fullers traveled as itinerant missionaries to the remote villages of the Western states. Fuller left the fruitpacking business and entered the Bible Institute of Los Angeles. He became a renowned Bible teacher in his community and formed a church from a small Bible class which he served for ten years. From the sanctuary of Calvary Church of Placentia, California, Fuller launched his radio ministry in 1925 over a single local radio station. He later became director of "The Old-Fashioned Revival Hour." The broadcast's joyful format gained immediate acceptance and enabled it to expand rapidly to other stations. During the 1940s Fuller also directed a large number of evangelists in many parts of North America through the Fuller Evangelistic Foundation. Meanwhile the Gospel Broadcasting Association continued to expand the Old Fashioned Revival Hour's coverage from North America to almost every spot on the globe. For fifteen years, beginning with World War II, the program was produced each Sunday afternoon from the Municipal Auditorium in Long Beach, California, where it drew huge audiences. At the time of Dr. Fuller's death in March 1968, the broadcast was heard on more than five hundred stations around the world.

## Comments on Ephesians 4:14

*It is dangerous for a Christian to lose interest in the great foundational truths of our faith because they have become familiar. This is one of the reasons for the many exhortations in the Word to "hold fast," "be steadfast," "watch and pray." And let me say this to you, that one of the outstanding essential works of a true, growing, deepening Christian life is to be stedfast, unmovable, "not carried about by every wind of doctrine." Such a Christian becomes strong because he is rooted and grounded, like a tree planted by the rivers of water, not merely set out for decorative purposes, but deeply rooted. We need warning against the peril of drifting.*

# Martin R. De Haan

## (1891–1965)

M. R. De Haan was born in Zeeland, Michigan, the son of a cobbler who had emigrated from the Netherlands. He graduated from Hope College in Holland, Michigan, and the University of Illinois College of Medicine. On June 25, 1914, he married Priscilla Venhuizen and soon became a successful physician in Western Michigan. The teaching of his godly parents bore fruit during a period of illness, when he sensed the distinct call to preach the Gospel. He gave up his medical practice and completed training at Western Theological Seminary in Holland, Michigan. He pastored two churches in Grand Rapids which grew rapidly under his clear and forceful preaching. The Lord endowed him with the ability to make Bible truth simple and easily understood. De Haan began sharing this gift with several large Bible classes, and in 1938 as an outgrowth of one of these classes in Detroit, the Lord led in the expansion of this teaching by means of radio. The program, known as the Radio Bible Class, grew rapidly and was soon heard over two national networks. In more than a quarter of a century, without ever appealing to the radio audience for funds, De Haan saw the broadcast grow under God's direction from a local venture on a fifty-watt station to a ministry of more than six hundred selected stations around the world. During those years he spoke at many Bible conferences across the country and wrote twenty-five books and numerous booklets. He edited and published a monthly devotional guide, *Our Daily Bread,* which has circulation of over eight hundred thousand. The entire literature production of the Radio Bible Class now exceeds a million pieces per month. On December 13, 1965, M. R. De Haan was called home to be with the Lord.

## From the Sermon, "The House of Blood"

*We see then that the tabernacle was indeed a "house of blood." But all of this blood was merely prophetic, typical, and a shadow of the blood of the coming Lamb of God. The blood of slain animals could not atone for sin. It could not take sin away. It could "cover" sin, for that is the meaning of "atonement," but it could not remove it, or reconcile man to God. The blood of animals could atone for sin, but only the blood of Christ could bring about "reconciliation" by propitiation.*

# CONCLUSION

Christianity swept into the twentieth century on a rising tide of evangelicalism which had produced mission societies, evangelical movements which crossed denominational barriers, and revivals. The spread of Christianity through the first years of this century was interrupted by World War I. In the years following World War I, there was much tension between nations, many small wars and revolutions, as well as another major world war, a police action in Korea, followed by Viet Nam. In addition to these events, increasing secularism undercut all denominations and made them all seem outmoded. Rapid scientific advance aided in producing religious skepticism. Communism was also spreading its atheistic message. All those factors weighed against Christianity.

Despite these disadvantages, the Christian faith spread throughout the world in this century. Although Biblical Christians were in the minority in Europe and America, the spread of Christianity across the world continued. In non-Western nations the faith was taking root in indigenous leadership and was growing from new Christian communities. Western missionaries were regarding themselves more as fellow-helpers in the work with national pastors, rather than as outsiders with a superiority attitude.

The twentieth century witnessed a movement for denominational unity, unknown in previous decades. This desire for unity grew into what is called the *Ecumenical Movement*. This movement and the institutionalization of denominations was challenged by Biblical Christianity. Other detrimental influences in Christianty were neo-orthodoxy in its various forms, neo-liberalism, religious secularism, and more recently, "the death of God" movement. Despite such "counter-movements" Biblical Christianity has continued to grow, and is now effecting the transformation of many lives by the power of God. As it enters the final third of the twentieth century, Christianity is faced with the challenge of relating its structure and timeless message to a rapidly changing society. These years present Christianity with its greatest challenge and its greatest opportunity.